CONCILIUM

THEOLOGY IN THE AGE OF RENEWAL

CONCILIUM

CONCILIUM/VOL. 35

MORAL THEOLOGY

THE
SOCIAL MESSAGE
OF THE
GOSPELS

edited by FRANZ BÖCKLE

Volume 35

CONCILIUM
theology in the age of renewal

PAULIST PRESS
NEW YORK, N.Y. / GLEN ROCK, N.J.

Library of Congress Catalogue Card Number: 68–31249

Suggested Decimal Classification: 261.8

Paulist Press assumes responsibility for the accuracy of the English translations in this Volume.

PAULIST PRESS
EXECUTIVE OFFICES: 304 W. 58th Street, New York, N.Y. and 21 Harris-
town Road, Glen Rock, N.J.
Executive Publisher: John A. Carr, C.S.P.
Executive Manager: Alvin A. Illig, C.S.P.
Asst. Executive Manager: Thomas E. Comber, C.S.P.

EDITORIAL OFFICES: 304 W. 58th Street, New York, N.Y.
Editor: Kevin A. Lynch, C.S.P.
Managing Editor: Urban P. Intondi

Printed and bound in the United States of America by
The Colonial Press Inc., Clinton, Mass.

CONTENTS

PART II

BIBLIOGRAPHICAL SURVEY

PART III

DOCUMENTATION CONCILIUM
Office of the Executive Secretary
Nijmegen, Netherlands

PREFACE

Franz Böckle/*Bonn, W. Germany*

Christians are constantly reproached with the fact that in 2,000 years they have not succeeded in carrying out their noble social principles. This harsh rebuke addressed to Christianity is in essence the expression of a great expectation. We are quite clearly expected to provide a constructive contribution to a just order of society and to the solution of ethical problems that constantly emerge.

The present volume is inspired by this expectation. We have to find out in what way the Church and her committed Christians help to mold the moral consciousness of our society and can influence the norms that guide social life. Social anthropology emphasizes the importance of binding norms for the social life of mankind. The so-called "theory of social change" points to the need for, as well as the conditions and other factors of, a development of these norms. Among these factors the Church must have her place. But what part must she play? Is her watchword "revolution" or "reform"?

We cannot find a specific social theory in the Bible, for it provides no argument in favor either of individualism or of collectivism. On the other hand, it is certain that the message of both the Old and the New Testaments is orientated toward the community. The Gospel is a social message in the best sense of that word. It has a liberating function in that it subjects the customary

1

norms of both the biblical and the non-biblical traditions to the criterion of brotherly love. Neither Jesus nor his apostles developed a concrete social and political program. But by preaching the equal value and dignity of every human person in Christ, early Christianity provided a new criterion and a powerful impulse toward a gradual transformation of society.

The fact that Christians themselves frequently did not take this criterion seriously, or that there were times when they denied in practice the social consequences of this criterion, makes one understand the many bitter objections made by atheists against Christianity, but it does not change the fact that despite everything the liberating force of the Gospel has persisted with increasing intensity. Saints and heretics alike often contributed more to achieve this result than the compromising action of the authorities. But it is altogether too simple if, looking back from the present understanding of man, one blames Christianity for every social evil. This is a highly unhistorical way of thinking which ignores the very complex and always necessary process of development.

It would seem obvious that, without the contribution of Christianity, the struggle about the worth of the human person is simply unthinkable. No philosophy has yet succeeded in finding a positive basis for the eternal and infinite worth of the human person. Only the revelation that an infinite God loves every man infinitely is for Christianity the basic guarantee of its certainty about the value of man. This is a rich possession which carries a heavy responsibility. This knowledge must be constantly applied to ever changing historical conditions. Here lies the heart of Christian ethics and of the social and political commitment of the Christian. Here lies the contribution which we are asked to make to a critical and constructive development of social norms. To do this meaningfully and with some measure of success we need:

1. A basic discussion of the culturally and historically conditioned understanding of man, in which the concrete norms of the human situation are rooted.

2. Exact knowledge of the factual problems without which it is impossible to have any concrete moral rules or any aid in decision-making.

3. A certain familiarity with the factors and laws that determine the development of social norms. In every culture the so-called change in the norms is subject to definite factors. Here empirical sociology has already provided us with valuable insights today. Only when we have become familiar with these laws is it possible for us to integrate our basic Christian views of the value and dignity of man into a given society as *maxims that really belong to it*. This might well be the sole, and is certainly the most promising, way of making a genuine contribution of our own. A mere repetition of old norms would be futile.

Christian social ethics cannot do without the aid of the social sciences, as I have already said. The way has often been blocked by misunderstandings. It is hoped that the informative contributions may help to dispose of prejudices and pave the way for better understanding.

PART I
ARTICLES

Wilhelm Korff/*Bonn, W. Germany*

Empirical Social Study and Ethics

Dialogue between moral theology and empirical social study has scarcely even started.[1] The reconciling of prejudices and misunderstandings is seriously hindered from both sides. On the one hand, the methods and conclusions of social study are written off as positivistic or relativistic; on

[1] This applies especially to dialogue on questions of methods and of scientific-theoretical self-understanding between moral theology and empirical social science. The fact that one science, as the case may be, takes up and uses concrete insights and research results of the other is by itself no vast indication that each respects the other as a genuine partner in the process of discovering truth and that they are mutually fully aware of each other, each being ready to be taught by the other in order to be able to rethink and test its own position. An example of this is provided by a discussion that has been going on since 1957 in the Protestant *Zeitschrift für Evangelische Ethik*. The discussion was sparked off in an essay by the sociologist Helmut Schelsky, "Ist die Dauerreflexion institutionalisierbar? Zum Thema einer modernen Religionssoziologie" (1957), pp. 153–74, and it is still going on. (Cf. the two last contributions by Reinhold Lindner, "Über die Zusammenarbeit von Soziologie und Theologie" [1966], pp. 65–80, and by Hubertus Diik de Loor, "Soziologie und Theologie" [1967], pp. 159–68.) The absence of such a dialogue in Catholic circles—at least in German-speaking countries—cannot be offset by the other positively valuable fact that Catholic moral theology is steadily becoming more and more ready to accept and assimilate the results of empirical social research, especially since the work of Werner Schöllgen, "Die soziologischen Grundlagen der katholischen Sittenlehre," in *Handbuch der katholischen Sittenlehre V*, edited by F. Tillmann (Düsseldorf, 1953). Schöllgen has produced numerous other essays which have given a mighty impetus along this direction.

the other, moral theology as a normative science is asked to explain how dogmatic assertions can be regarded as scientific statements in any sense at all.

The purpose of this article is to overcome prejudices and give an honest answer to genuine questions, for today the two disciplines are thrown back upon one another in a high degree as the human environment becomes more complex. What is required is not just study and observation, but regulation and formation as well. This article is designed to provide initial methodological orientation. In the process it will investigate especially the question of how far the committed or dogmatically formed reason can expect help from the empirical outlook. The discussion will center, therefore, upon the two disciplines of social science, the practical function of which is undisputed, but the integration of which into ethics is still ultimately unaccomplished. These disciplines are *sociology* and—the youngest member of the family of social studies—*social cybernetics.*

I

THE PROBLEMS FACING SOCIOLOGY

Sociology sees its essential function as the investigation of social data in their causal interconnection. The core of its method consists in the exposition and comparison of social data which can be seen to stand in a causal relation to the social phenomenon requiring explanation. The data, for their part, must be verifiable. Hence, as a rule they are established by means of a special empirical proceeding (observation, interview, statistics and appeal to evidence that is assured historically and critically, ethnologically and archaeologically). Characterizing this method briefly, we might say that it concerns the elaboration of theories about social phenomena in the light of hypotheses and their empirical verification.

Admittedly, such a way of proceeding is necessarily selective. In other words, in the explication of the causal context of a social phenomenon, not every conceivable factor is taken into account. Chiefly to be ignored is the wealth of factors that are important merely at the level of individual history, and which, although significant for social structure, are without consequence. Attention must rather be paid to those factors which, on account of their specific socially binding claims, are able to precipitate further social effects, and only those will be examined which imply a causal connection on account of their frequent or regular parallel appearance along with the phenomenon under inquiry. The validity of sociological theories is based solely upon the empirical material which verifies them. This fact compels the sociologist constantly to submit his assumptions to control and correction. On the other hand, it also allows him freedom, when the occasion arises, to select from the factors in question for the purpose of examining *special* interdependencies. A classic example of this is Max Weber's theory concerning the significance of Calvinist ethics for the rise of modern capitalism. Without forfeiting conviction, this theory sets aside other relevant factors such as the presupposition of a technical and scientific civilization.[2]

II

THE INFORMATION VALUE OF SOCIOLOGICAL THEORIES

This method of producing theories, which enables us to illumine many-sided and complex social phenomena by reference to their causal context, replaces slogans, unproved presumptions and oversimplified explanations by demonstrable assertions that can be checked against empirical findings. Responsible practi-

[2] On the methodological problem of the production of sociological theories, we refer especially to the following basic works: E. Durkheim, *Les Règles de la méthode sociologique* (Paris, 1895), chapter 6; F. Simiand, *La méthode positive en science économique* (Paris, 1912); *ibid., Le salaire, L'évolution sociale et la monnaie*, 3 vols. (Paris, 1932), esp. the Introduction, chapters 1–4; cf. also R. Dahrendorf, *Gesellschaft und Freiheit* (Munich, 1965), pp. 33–43.

tioners in politics, economics and social life, from whom reliable
and useful decisions are expected, have long since been convinced
of the information value of such theories. Today the science of
sociology has established itself outside the universities, above all
as "commissioned research", precisely because of its value in
practice. By contrast, the assistance this science could give to the
formation of judgment and to planning in the Church's pastoral
sphere has, for the most part, not yet been sufficiently recognized.

Meanwhile, with the additional help provided by modern
cybernetics, even more advanced methods have been developed
that not only permit the *analysis* of social phenomena, but enable
us to *prognosticate* empirically future tendencies in social processes. This opens up the way for the planned, rationalized and
"effectivity-orientated" direction of man by man—a possibility
that seems to bring with it completely new moral problems. We
will have to conclude these discussions of method by adding a
few remarks elucidating the ethical situation in particular. These
remarks are in complete harmony with the views of the author of
the following article on social cybernetics. But now let us deal
first of all with the theme of sociology.

III

SOCIOLOGY AS A CRITIQUE OF IDEOLOGY

By a strict attachment to the controllable reality of social experience, sociology sets its own limits. For its theories it claims
no more and no less truth and validity than the recognized and
relevant data warrant. Thus it is fundamentally distinguished
from the doctrinaire interpretation of history and of society
which, refusing the decisive guidance and correction of experience, projects its particular insights into the flux of historical and
social processes, endowing these insights with absolute validity.
It is precisely with an eye on such theories—one calls to mind
the pauperization theory of doctrinaire Marxism or the race
theories backed by Darwinism—that sociology acquires, from

the level of the facts themselves, its inalienable function of debunking and destroying. On the basis of its empirical method it performs the function of necessary and effective criticism of ideology.

To this context also belongs the critical service that comparative cultural sociology can perform for modern ethics and moral theology. Thanks to its methodologically-based systematic research and stock-taking of the extraordinarily varied concepts of moral order that have become socially effective among men, we can now make precise statements about the actual extent and validity of material moral norms. Hence this sociological special discipline becomes the competent court to judge all the empirical arguments—that is, arguments appealing to experience and affecting the eternity of the moral law and of natural law, which hitherto have been used one way or the other within the sphere of ethics.[8]

IV

Moral Neutrality as a Working Norm of Sociology

In contrast to the normative sciences, empirical social study, like all empirical science, is neutral and non-tendentious in method. Whether the object of investigation is a burning issue or merely of academic interest, whether its selection depends upon the initiative of the inquirer or results from the commission

---

[8] F. X. Kaufmann in particular, in his pioneer study in the field of the empirical foundations of natural law—"Die Ehe in sozialanthropologischer Sicht," in *Das Naturrecht im Disput*, ed. F. Böckle (Düsseldorf, 1966), pp. 15–60—points out the "culturally specific determinacy" (p. 47) of material ethical norms, but also asserts emphatically that the number of data which can be rationally regulated in only one way in all civilizations—such regulation being necessary for the survival of the civilization—is proved empirically to be very small: "As examples we need go no further than the incest taboo within the immediate family and the existence of the family itself. Another norm of this type is possibly the prohibition of murder and, even more, of cannibalism within the group, which, according to Gehlen, found its first moral sanction in totemism" (p. 52).

of an interested group, the method is not affected in the slightest. Sociology is indeed concerned with value judgments and norms of behavior, but it does not itself make these judgments or affirm these norms. All it does is to find out what is. The normative character attached to the phenomena is totally irrelevant to the explication of the connection between these phenomena, insofar as the analysis is confined purely to the demonstration of empirical similarities, dependencies and tendencies. To this extent the so-called principle of "moral neutrality"—i.e., refraining from passing judgment, as a condition of sociological knowledge—first formulated distinctly by Max Weber in 1914, is completely justified.[4]

This principle, which exclusively affirms the requisite scientific working rules ensuring the objectivity of the process of research, and which as such has nothing to say either for or against the necessity of value judgments outside the sphere of this method, by no means renders superfluous the conscious involvement of the human intelligence that is directing proceedings. This is proved most clearly by the fact that both the selection of the object of research and also the appraising of the results (i.e., the practical assessment of the results) plainly represent interested, value-accented and, as such, morally responsible processes. These processes lie, it is true, outside the scope of method, but they are *directly and constitutively* related to it—anteriorly or retrospectively.

In regard to these two poles, the specifically ethical problematic of the method emerges in exactly the same way as it does for

---

[4] On the history of the controversy about moral evaluation in regard to the present state of the discussion, cf. R. Dahrendorf, *op. cit.,* pp. 27–48; *Logik der Sozialwissenschaften,* ed. E. Topitsch (Cologne-Berlin, 1965), articles by: C. von Ferber, "Der Werturteilsstreit 1909/1959. Versuch einer wissenschaftsgeschichtlichen Interpretation," pp. 165–80; H. Albert, "Wertfreiheit als methodisches Prinzip. Zur Frage der Notwendigkeit einer normativen Sozialwissenschaft," pp. 181–210; J. Habermas, "Analytische Wissenschaftstheorie und Dialektik," pp. 291–311; R. Mayntz, "Soziologie in der Eremitage? Kritische Bemerkurgen zum Vorwurf des Konservatismus der Soziologie," pp. 526–41, as well as the bibliography on this problem, pp. 548–49.

all empirical study, especially the natural sciences, except that there it often appears in a much more radical form. Whatever it may be that forever urges man on to acquire fresh knowledge, whether and how far it is good for him to acquire such knowledge, and whatever he does with it for good or ill, the rationality of the empirical sciences maintains complete indifference toward the possible consequences of its own application. The question of the morality of the moral neutrality of science is thrown back upon those who exploit science.

V

MORAL NEUTRALITY AS A POSITIVISTIC NORM OF THOUGHT

However, we must take a very different view of the positivistic notion which, illicitly extending the application of the principle as a scientific working norm, exalts it into a norm of thought, thus giving academic sanction to a relativism which ultimately allows one "to condemn the evil practices of a totalitarian regime as little as the curious marriage customs of a primitive tribe".[5] Such a view implies that, having made our empirical statements, we have reached the ultimate limit of what can be stated scientifically, and it denies all scientific character to the normative disciplines. It would be quite unjust to the processes of evaluation—without which there would be no social structures and regulative ordinances at all (the existence of which none disputes)—were we to follow the spirit of this sociological concept, which sees science as tied purely to phenomena, and relegate these processes of evaluation to the realm of a pre-scientific subjectivity that never becomes amenable to reason.

Self-knowledge simply refuses to deny that reason is also at work in evaluation, and that this reason is elucidative and creative. But it is this very fact, indeed, that permits us to make evaluation as such, and hence the inner validity, truth and reason

---

[5] Barrington Moore, Jr., *Political Power and Social Theory* (Cambridge 1958), chapter 3, quoted by R. Mayntz, *op. cit.,* p. 534.

of whatever exhibits itself as a sociological phenomenon, into an object of special reflection that is specifically concerned with regulating behavior. Applied science, and especially philosophical and theological ethics which have explicated this applied science in terms of its unifying meaning and foundation, have always sought to do this. However, to trace reason back to the blind rationality of phenomena, as positivism attempts, involves no less than its total moral abdication; it is the affirmation of its incompetence to give any foundation at all to human responsibility.[6]

---

* It is quite a different question whether the problem of the appraising and action-directing reason and the real experience upon which this is based are illumined by the categorial basis of the concept of value in general, and whether in the end the problem of positivism leads toward a solution. Hitherto it has been too little recognized that Max Weber has interpreted this concept, which he introduced into empirical social research. This interpretation strongly bears the stamp of the neo-Kantian epistemology of Heinrich Rickert. (Cf. H. Rickert, *Die Grenzen der naturwissenschaftlichen Begriffsbildung*. In the Foreword to the fourth edition of 1921, p. xxiii, as in the postscript to the fifth edition of 1928, p. 758, Rickert explicitly points out Weber's dependence upon him.) In the concept of value, Rickert tried to preserve that which is negated by the natural scientific concept of reality, and then to legitimize its scientific analysis in the concept of "value reference". Weber then took from Rickert the important distinction that values do not *exist* but *have validity*. It is precisely this ontologically unexplained dualism which may have paved the way for a sociological understanding of value. But even the anti-neo-Kantian theory of value expounded in the phenomenological ethics of Max Scheler and Nikolai Hartmann is not able to provide a satisfactory solution to the central problem of the reason that concretely controls action and hence, as occasion requires, creates moral norms. It is true that the ethics of value, assisted by the concept of "sense of purpose", is able to defeat the positivistic account and exhibit the intrinsic validity of values over against a merely neutral and utilitarian claim to currency. However, in order to provide this attribute of validity with ontological foundation, they must lay claim to a transcendence of reality; a validity that is independent of consciousness must claim a validity "in itself", a timeless "ideal being" (N. Hartmann). In the last analysis, history alone can allow this to emerge—even on the part of man who perceives these values. On this argument the dimension of "the normative" cannot be introduced into the concept of value, nor can it be established from it. But this dimension is constitutive for actual ethics as the science which reflects man's practical action and in the process exhibits itself as a science that regulates action. In this it distinguishes itself from antecedent descriptive sociology, as also from the *a priori* value researches of

VI

THE PROBLEM OF THE NORMATIVE POWER OF THE FACTUAL

Nothing, however, seems to encourage the leveling of moral reason down to the mere rationality of phenomena so much as the "normative power of the factual"—an indisputable empirical phenomenon. Placed in tension between normative and empirical judgment, no other process within the field of human behavior is so acutely vulnerable to misunderstanding, and no other so urgently needs a sober, methodically reliable interpretation.

Sociologically, the above-cited formula, which sums up the phenomenon in a catch-phrase, first of all means no more than that an actual behavior pattern becoming dominant within a society is able to supplant ancient norms and assume binding validity for itself. From this we conclude that this process may be regarded as one of the possible ways in which a change in values can come about. Closer analysis of the phenomenon reveals that for a practice deviating from the norm to have a chance of becoming a normative rule, it must increasingly be felt and proclaimed to be *more correct*—i.e., its rivalry with the existent norm must be supported by legitimacy. More precisely, the formula about the "normative power of the factual" applies not to the simple fact that the behavior of the majority runs counter to the norm, but to the qualified fact that such a majority willingly identify themselves with their own actual behavior. The current order remains unassailed as long as conviction in it remains—"even if the righteous falls seven times a day".[7] For this very reason, every attempt to overthrow a moral order by unmasking its non-observance is doomed to recoil upon itself as long as none doubt the reasonableness of that order.

However, this does not exclude the possibility that knowledge of the spread of morally deviant behavior, itself claiming the

---

the phenomenologists who leave unanswered the Kantian question—What ought we to do?—and are unable even to provide a fresh code of values themselves.

[7] Cf. F. K. Francis, *Wissenschaftliche Grundlagen soziologischen Denkens* (Bern, 1957), pp. 105f.

support of increasing rationality and hence legitimacy, might certainly encourage general readiness to test former convictions and hence also encourage openness to reorientation and change of norms. In this case we would have to assess exactly the part played in the processes of a change in social norms "from beneath" by, for example, modern opinion polls and statistical inquiries. Thus we have already stumbled upon the ambivalent effect of neutral social research. It is true that the intention behind such research is to do no more than uncover and analyze facts, but when the results are published people take sides and allow conclusions to influence their actions, so that in the end the normative structures of behavior may be altered. As we said, responsibility for this effect cannot be laid upon the empirical method, which itself proclaims no norms, but merely seeks to elucidate the empirical data upon which the factual validity of given norms already rests.

This sociological analysis of the phenomenon of the "normative power of the factual"—which at this point would have to take particular account of the specifically indirect but powerful influence of empirical social research upon the processes of the changing of norms—provides us with the criteria that enable us to deal with the plainly ideological consequences drawn from the phenomenon. First among such ideological consequences we list the totally inadequate attempt to fundamentally solve the problem of norms upon the basis of this phenomenon. This tendency is shown above all by the well-known Kinsey Report and others like it, which operate by means of statistical data about attitudes to sex life in industrial society. By postulating a gradual adaptation of socially accepted norms to actual, sometimes statistically ascertainable, behavior, the "normative power of the factual" seems to worm its way into the position of a universal imperative, a *norma normans*.

Setting aside the naive biologism of this report, which with its postulate of a "natural" indulgence of human impulses completely fails to see the vital importance of normative structures for the civilization to which man's own *nature* urges him,[8] its chief error lies in its immediate imputation of normative power to any sheer datum of behavior that deviates from the norm, without taking any account of the verdict of the person interrogated concerning his own action.[9] But the assimilation of norms in the name of practice, without knowing whether or not those who so practice approve of what they practice, quite defies logic. All of this is very far from a scientific ethical assessment of the specific phenomenon.

It is just such an exposition as this—finding considerable support despite its lack of logic—that explains the growing conservative distrust of the subject matter under inquiry. This in turn leads to a further contrary misinterpretation. Without properly finding out about the specific structure of the phenomenon, some feel that the primacy of moral reason is fundamentally threatened by the "normative power of the factual", and that its claim to direct is forfeited in face of the realities of behavior. Anxiety is heightened by the added suspicion that the universal validity of moral norms in general is being threatened. And so, those who think thus feel themselves obliged to regard these developments as a form of moral decline and to denounce this method of establishing moral and social norms as quite inadmissible. If, however, in contrast we take as our basis not a prejudice born of its ideological counterpart, but the real structure of the phenomenon as revealed by sober sociological analysis, both of these anxieties vanish. Then—let us repeat—it will always be only the conviction inherent in an actual mode of behavior that will press for social recognition and, as such, will develop, as a normative force. In order to obviate misunderstanding, in the future we should therefore speak rather of the *"normative power of actually lived conviction"*. However, one would hardly deny all rational-

---

[8] This is expounded especially by H. Schelsky, "Die Moral der Kinsey-Reporte," in *Wort und Wahrheit* 6 (1954); also cf. *ibid.*, *Soziologie der Sexualität* (Hamburg, 1955), pp. 51ff.

[9] Attention has already been drawn to this error of method by F. X. Kaufmann, *op. cit.*, p. 48.

ity *a priori* to convictions merely on the ground that they already determine life, even before they have become socially sanctioned moral demands or been made legitimate as operative legal norms.

Classic ethical tradition has always been aware of this potential rationality of the factual and has positively accepted and honored the processes of discovering and creating norms "from beneath". Aristotle considered this to be the *"ethos"*, which was the essence of the unwritten ordinances governing the life of a society, and which preceded all the codified ordinances of the *"nomos"*. The latter found all its content in the former, and without the former it would have no power to demand obedience.[10] St. Thomas took up these facts anew in his concept of *"consuetudo"* as the most practiced, constant manner of behavior. W. Kluxen has probably touched on the essential core of the doctrine of *consuetudo* as it affects our problem when he sums up: "The fact of customary action contains as much power to form history as does formal law, if that action predominates in society. It possesses law-giving and law-establishing effect, or represents at least a constant exposition of the law." [11] However, both formal legislation and the "factually lived conviction" of *consuetudo* are exposed to the alternatives of *progress* or *decline;* along these the demands of moral reason may be either fulfilled or denied. At this point, however, the further one-sided reproach against our phenomenon disappears—the reproach that it threatens the universal validity of moral norms, for the same reproach would have to be made of formal law. In fact, the problem of coordinating supratemporally valid and historically conditioned normativity—and today there is no more burning issue—has no place at all within the framework of questions dealing solely with weighing up the empirically possible ways of creating norms. The confusion of these two essentially different complexes of

[10] *Pol.* II 1269 a 20–24 and *Pol.* III 1287 b 5. On this, cf. J. Ritter, *Naturrecht bei Aristoteles* (Stuttgart, 1961), pp. 23f.

[11] W. Kluxen, *Philosophische Ethik bei Thomas von Aquin* (Mainz, 1964), p. 241; cf. St. Thomas, *Summa Theol.* I–II, 97. Correctly, Kluxen stresses: "The concept of custom announces the whole problem of 'ethos', in all its aspects—historical, sociological, political and pedagogic."

problems can only be detrimental to both and, as was made clear above, can lead only to ideological consequences.

VII

MAN CONTROLLING MAN:
SOCIAL CYBERNETICS AS AN ETHICAL PROBLEM

Our reflections up to this point have centered on the problem of the ways a society remolds and establishes norms. Now we are left to face the problematic already suggested in the concept of social cybernetics: By what means do social aspirations, norms and values, which have already emerged as possessing an unequivocal claim to currency, effectively reach the individual and organize him? We now come face to face with man's historical situation. He is the heir to thoughts, feelings, imperatives and beliefs that come from before him and from outside himself, and all this is what now lays its claim upon him.

The situation is chiefly that of an heir to a cultural reality, and the individual always sees himself as set within the stream of its tradition and as growing into it. He lets himself be possessed, convinced and formed by it; by making it his own he receives from it an attitude, a structure, a profile, and ultimately it determines the modes of his understanding of himself and of the world.

But he is also heir to a behavior pattern which as an individual he accepts and which—more importantly—takes him over as it were. This behavior pattern, of which human beings are the living vehicle, itself develops an active and determining power, for at each point in time it is effectively present and socially sanctioned. The human observer seeks to gain control of this power, to become incorporated in it and accommodated to it, and this power, for the sake of its own functionality, lays claims upon him, sets norms for him and appoints roles for him to play.

Finally, in regard to our specifically modern pluralistic culture, the situation is (not least) the normative cognitive situation of one who knows himself to be wooed and addressed by a multiplicity of intrinsically consistent and—insofar as they operate upon the same level of intention—mutually competitive institutions and functional systems—systems which try to influence and persuade him and all potential consumers, fellow-workers, electors and faithful.

In virtue of this intermittent social and cultural influence and molding—and this is where empirical social research comes in—the individual as a civilized being for the first time becomes amenable to specific cultural generalization and appears as subsumed under a class; his actions can be empirically grasped, tabulated, calculated and prognosticated in terms of positively given and namable influencing factors. To this extent the fact that human behavior is predominantly directed from without—to use a phrase of David Kiesman's—creates the structural preconditions for the possibility of those generalizing methods and procedures which modern social science has developed, both for the purpose of *research* and also for that of *guiding* human action. The latter means that the social and cultural influencing and molding of mankind, his direction and education toward given social norms concerning what is expected of him, becomes the object of purposeful planning. Indeed, this can be more efficiently arranged to the degree in which all the motivating and influencing factors, which prepare and condition mankind to open up to the current touch of the controlling helm, are recognized and made operative.

The actual necessity of this kind of rationalized mode of guiding man by man is to be found, on the one hand, in the consequence of the free pluralistic modern civilization and of the competitive principle implied in it, and, on the other hand, in the consequence of the integrating collective system which we find in any highly specialized industrial society, one of the conditions of which is a supply of men who are both highly adaptable and highly specialized.

It is not easy to find specific criteria by which to explicate the ethical situation in all this, especially as the development of this process of collective planning, programming and guiding, as already adumbrated upon the basis of social economic, sociological, and social psychological, empirical research, entered upon its most decisive phase only with the advent of modern cybernetics. Nevertheless, I think that distinctions can be provided that make at least a fundamental ethical point of view possible.

First, following Hermann Lübbe, we might point out that modern (Western) planning technology does not work from the standpoint of an historically total conception of human existence, but merely from partial viewpoints, "preferring to follow the pragmatic rather than the teleological form of progress". "Man as the *subject* of such planning, in the totality of his subjectivity, remains outside the planner's full reckoning. As the *object* of the planning, he is never regarded except partially, whether as the socially insured, the businessman, the potential 'A' level candidate or what you will." [12]

We may not ignore the fact, however, that planning and direction are often carried out in such a way that, although the viewpoint is certainly partial, ethically the process is seriously deficient. Certain forms of modern advertising of consumer goods, for example, show how guidance can in truth be plainly guidance by an interested party—nothing but a system-orientated manipulation. And so we conclude that this pragmatic planning based on partial aspects of man does not possess any built-in moral reason.

On the other hand, however, and in complete contrast to this, we also know of a form of guidance that does not suffer the limitation of partiality and that is ethically perfectly legitimate. This guidance sees man in his authentic subjectivity and the meaning of his being; it aims at "his whole soul, his whole mind and all of his faculties". It sees him as oriented toward God. The Church has a permanent responsibility for this ultimate orienta-

[12] H. Lübbe, "Herrschaft und Planung. Die Veränderte Rolle der Zukunft in der Gegenwart," in *Die Frage nach dem Menschen. Festschrift für Max Müller,* ed. H. Rombach (Munich, 1966), pp. 188–211, esp. p. 208. This contains a bibliography on the problem of social-technological planning and futurology.

tion of man, and this orientation has to do with the "totality of his subjectivity", to use Lübbe's phrase.

It is true that even the Church can fulfill this function only in an earthly and historical fashion. She must concretize the task in a host of finite objectives and, in so doing, use finite means. To this extent she, too, is always of necessity thrown back upon the mode of partiality and hence, in turn, upon the method of programming and planning.

What, then, transforms partial control into ethically justified control? This is probably the heart of the problem that faces ecclesiastical and secular control alike. The answer depends essentially upon the *intention* behind the structure of the process of control. Therefore, it should be phrased: Control of man by man is moral only when both the objective of the control and the corresponding content of the control methods used are morally justified.

At this point it immediately becomes plain that it cannot be the determining power of a purposeful entity as such which destroys the moral autonomy of those who approve of it, and that thus it is not the modern control processes as such, designed to produce results, which debase and corrupt the inner moral structure of the act of assent and approval. In principle this applies indeed to the social cybernetic process designed to achieve the more efficient management of collective persuasion, just as it applies to the whole range of depth-psychological, socio-psychological and pedagogic techniques aimed at the individual. The thing that can be defective or despicable is, rather, the norm which the control hopes to establish, or the intentional content of the means used to win the assent of the mind or—more concretely—used to seduce the mind into assent and approval, whether these means be cunning, deceit, persuasion or coercion.

Having made this first attempt to provide ethical illumination of the problem of control—and we have to refrain from detailed casuistry on account of lack of space—let us pose a final strictly practical question, which may serve as a transition to the following article: In the sphere of the Church's pastoral and missionary work, dare we any longer turn our back upon the possibilities provided by the modern technology of planning and by social cybernetics?

It is true that meanwhile the empirical methods of sociology and ethnology as instruments of stock-taking and critical analysis have been more and more assimilated, but the collective control procedures, first developed in the economic sphere, have not been assimilated—although, in contrast, there has been a pastoral application of psychotherapy in techniques of influencing and educating the individual. In the collective sphere, however, the fear of illegitimate, functionalist manipulation and a falsely understood concept of freedom—basically positivistic and atomized —present many still insuperable obstacles. Here freedom is falsely understood not as the transcendental foundation perpetually and immediately given in man's "relation to himself", but as "something *beside* man" [18]—ultimately, that is, as a wider *determinatio* for which, in this view, a field of play must be left open within the whole system of determinants.

What has been said about the concept of freedom applies analogously to the concept of grace which, as man's deliberate turning toward God, must be seen in the closest connection with the intentional character of freedom. This means that grace, like freedom, as a specifically transcendental event, cannot be factorized. The clear division between *intentio* and *determinatio* might also help to remove the distrust of the phenomenon of rationalized control in the pastoral sphere.

[18] J. B. Metz, "Freiheit als philosophisch-theologisches Grenzproblem," in *Gott in Welt. Festgabe für Karl Rahner*, 1 (Freiburg/Basel/Vienna, 1964), pp. 287–314, esp. p. 296.

Roger Garaudy/*Chennevières, France*

What Does a Non-Christian Expect of the Church in Matters of Social Morality?

What the non-Christian expects the Church to contribute to the formation and development of norms of public morality will necessarily depend on the image of Christianity suggested by the attitude of the Church herself, the theologians and Christians at large in this second half of the 20th century.

The most striking feature of this modern Christianity seems to me to be that it is a Christianity on the move. If, then, we want to say what we hope of this Christianity, we must first try to describe the transformation we are witnessing, to pin down the direction in which we believe this advance is moving, and to imagine what further development we may not merely await but intensely hope for, because it is on this orientation that the possibility of fulfilling man's highest vocation together will in large measure depend.

The Transformation of Christianity

One of the most positive results of Vatican Council II has been to put man at the heart of its preoccupation and thus encourage the development of a theology of earthly values. This orientation expresses a movement which is common to the whole of Christianity, both Catholic and Protestant, in this second half of the 20th century.

limiting man's responsibility or his creative power through a radical initiative which nothing in man foreshadows or calls for, apart from the negation of his adequacy.

This problem is now frankly tackled by Christian theologians and philosophers who are taking up the challenge to the faith thrown down by atheistic humanism. In his fine book, *El cristianismo no es un humanismo* (Barcelona, 1966), J. M. Gonzalez-Ruiz powerfully stressed the "gratuitousness" of the God of the Bible at the level of knowledge; he is not an answer that is immanent to the problems of man, and at the level of action grace does not interfere with nature. Only thus is God not a rival of man's creative energy. He exposes the twofold error of either making grace intervene at the level of immanence in order to find a religious answer for the problems of science, technology, morality or politics, which would be a denial of the autonomy of human values, or of accepting an "inflated transcendence" which would put all genuine values beyond this world and thus take the meaning out of human history from which the spirit must turn away in order to fulfill its vocation. In both cases, atheistic humanism—the atheism of Marx—is right in thinking that such a conception would paralyze man's effort.

Vatican Council II provided an analysis of the two basic objections of atheistic humanism: (1) religion casts doubt on man's autonomy; (2) the eschatological experience puts a brake on man's full unfolding in history.

That, historically speaking, Christianity deserves these two reproaches can hardly be contested. However, the problem is not to start a controversy about the past but rather to find out whether this alienating role is of the essence of the faith.

Gonzalez-Ruiz says: "Grace is not an intruder whose role it is to outshine the epic grandeur of Prometheus" (p. 31). "The humanism," he writes (p. 23), "which we are analyzing calls itself atheistic because it thinks that the 'Promethean' vocation of man is incompatible with the admission of God. Paul Ricoeur boldly concludes from a profound understanding of the Bible: 'In contrast with Greek thought, Christianity does not condemn

WHAT DOES A NON-CHRISTIAN EXPECT OF THE CHURCH? 25

This elaboration of a new, specifically Christian humanism has been made possible by a profound reflection on transcendence. It seems to me that everything started with Karl Barth who delivered a decisive blow at dogmatism in theology. This critical aspect of Barth's work may be compared to Kant's "Copernican revolution" in philosophy. Over against all theological dogmatism—i.e., all pretense of installing oneself in God's place and speaking in his name—Barth opposed the basic principle of all critical thinking—namely that whatever is said abou God, it is only man who says it.

This awareness of a radical discontinuity puts the problem o transcendence in the most acute light: God is truly "totally other" he is not a prolongation of our reason or of our values. It allow of no common language, no common morality. The false d lemma of Plato's *Eutyphron* has been cut: "Is an act good," aske Socrates, "because God willed it, or did God will it because it w: good?" This was confusing the human word with the divine, pr tending that man could catch God's initiative in the net of hum: reason. The last attempt in that direction was made by Heg who reduced God ultimately to being merely the whole of hum history, and by the same token perverted human history by m: ing it a simple and apparently temporal unfolding of a pre-ex ing totality, that of the spirit. This diminished God by adjust him to any given stage of the development of reason, and diminished man by depriving him of his limitless potential renewal and creation.

In his commentary on the Epistle to the Romans, Barth m tained against Hegel "what Kierkegaard calls the infinite q tative difference between time and eternity". Thereby he guarded to the full both the rights of God and the rights of 1 Only when God is truly God, the "totally other" of utter scendence, can man be fully man. If there is continuity bet God and man, all that is granted to the one is necessarily away from the other. But if there is no possible common me that can be applied to both, history becomes a creation for man is totally responsible, and God can then meet man w

Prometheus. For the Greeks, Prometheus' fault lay in having stolen the fire of technology and the arts, the fire of knowledge and of conscience. Adam's fault was not that of Prometheus; his disobedience did not consist in wanting to be a man of science and learning but in having broken the vital link with the divine in his human venture.' The readmission of Prometheus in the Christian calendar can only be achieved after serious thought about the God of the Bible." The problem is important because what an atheistic humanist awaits and hopes for is essentially that Christianity will fully rehabilitate Prometheus.

Gonzalez-Ruiz proceeds to do just this and thus has contributed to breaking down a major obstacle in the dialogue between Christians and Marxists: "The divine presence in the evolution of the cosmos and of man is totally gratuitous; it can only be perceived by an explicit revelation of God himself."

Over against "a deism manipulated in the interests of a dominant class" and thus turning God into "a mere cog in the wheel of the cosmos and of society", Ruiz maintains that "this stop-gap god recedes as man continues, by his own progress, to throw light on the obscure regions of ignorance and impotence. . . . The retreat of this 'god' is an indispensable condition for man's ascent, since this 'god' has become a rival of man." Starting from these two principles, "the uselessness of an hypothesis of God for the explanation of man's problems, and the power of man's self-creativeness, it is possible to humbly offer the world the service of evangelization."

Ruiz continues: "A Christianity that is ready to fight against any form of religious alienation cannot be an obstacle to the common attempt to bring about the integration of the ascending movement of man's activity" (p. 122). "It is man's task to create history by a constant effort to realize himself to the full and to humanize nature. Thus one sees that, in the religion of the Bible, the religious dimension of man lies precisely in his total responsibility for this humanizing evolution of the cosmos" (p. 33). In his Preface, M.-D. Chenu shows that it is this "theology of the world" which provided the material for the conciliar text of the

Pastoral Constitution on the Church in the Modern World. This gives us the measure of the importance of the step which the Church is taking and enables us to express the hope we base on it.

The possibility of this new humanism is born of the recognition of the autonomy of earthly values. First, there is the autonomy of science. God, as Fr. Dubarle quipped, is not the small supplement to our mental deficiencies. If morality is entitled to intervene in order to determine a scale of urgency in projects for research and must intervene in order to judge the human value of the application of science as leading to man's development or to his destruction, it has, no more than theology, the right to intervene in the free deployment of research as such.

Second, there is the specific and autonomous value of activity for the transformation and humanization of a world which itself has its own and autonomous value. Teilhard de Chardin's optimism with regard to what the world can become by man's effort, his exaltation of work, technology and scientific research, foreshadows that "theology of work" of which Chenu wrote: "Work carries on the work of the creator, and God continues to be present in the world by transforming it through the workers."

Thus man and the world of man have become the central preoccupation of the Christian in post-conciliar theology. As Karl Rahner said: "The question of man is the whole of dogmatic theology."

The Direction in Which This Advance Is Moving

One might object that this attitude is not so terribly new in Christianity. This is true. But this orientation toward man and the world has in fact often been obscured in Christian thought by the Greek dualism which reigned practically supreme from the 4th to the 20th centuries and which turned Christianity into what Nietzsche called, with justified contempt, "a Platonism for the people".

To teach that this world is but a temporary structure, that "the true life is elsewhere", beyond this life and beyond history, made Christianity, as Rimbaud said, "the eternal value of human forces", or, as Marx put it, "the opium of the people". This was hardly encouraging man to transform the world. It rather made him disdain the world and resign himself to the iniquities of this "vale of tears" where man was allotted but a brief stay while awaiting the "beyond".

It is true that the God of the Bible does not know a spiritual kingdom separate from the kingdom of this earth. It is also true that it was Stoic philosophy and not the Bible that extolled an "inward" freedom, severed from the external and material conditions of freedom. But it is also true that the history of Christianity shows only a few occasions when man was told to transform the world first in order to create the material conditions for a spiritual life. When such an appeal was launched, it was condemned as a heresy, from the *circumcellions* of the 4th century to Thomas Münzer of the 16th century. And when, outside the Church and against the Church, revolutions were organized in order to humanize man's world by putting an end to the old privileges and the old injustices, they were invariably condemned as diabolical, from the French Revolution of 1789 to those of 1848, from the Commune of Paris to the October Revolution. Only in the second half of the 20th century did some begin—and then still with great timidity—to become aware of the fact that "spiritualism" is the heresy which caused the worst breaks between the Church and the people.

Lucien Laberthonnière, whose brief and incisive essay on "Christian Realism and Greek Idealism" was significantly reprinted after Vatican Council II with such great success, was a pioneer in this attempt to dissociate Christianity from that traditional dualism. Pursuing this effort to disentangle Christianity from its Greek heritage, whether that of Plato or Aristotle, of the Stoa or of Plotinus, a Catholic philosopher, Leslie Dewart, tried to extend this distinction between what is fundamental to faith and the institutional or cultural forms of religion in his great work, *The Future of Belief*.

A similar movement is taking place in Protestant thought. Since Karl Barth taught the present generation of theologians that religion is often the last battlefield where man struggles against God and tries to make God something less than the sovereign of the whole of life, it is the very notion of "religion" (as opposing an "other world" to this one) that is queried in the name of faith. Dietrich Bonhoeffer was the first to speak of a "Christianity without religion", and a Protestant philosopher, Paul Ricoeur, defined "religion" as "alienation from faith".

Linked with this movement to disentangle what is basic in faith from the cultural forms which religion assumed at the various stages of its historical development is the work done on the "demythologization" of faith, inaugurated by Bultmann.

Kerygma and Myth

The keynote of Bultmann's work—namely that the faith must necessarily be expressed in the language, ways of thought, conception of the world and philosophy of a given era and society—can hardly be questioned. The most some of his Catholic critics, like Malevez and Caffarana, have been able to ask, and this rightly, is whether the myth is not bound to be the language of the kerygma. If the *concept* expresses and dominates an already existing reality, must the myth not be the expression of a reality which does not yet exist, the language of a promise and a call? But if man can only express this call of the transcendent in the language of myth, art and poetry, how can he decipher this demand of God?

As Barth says, the initiative can only come from God. But how can we recognize it? For too long this intervention of God was only seen in the gaps of natural causality, the miracle, or the failures and weaknesses of our reason, our power or our will. When, asked Bonhoeffer, shall we look for God not in the inadequacies, the misery and the weaknesses of man, but in the farthest reaches of man's achievement, the vanguard of human creativeness, and the strength and the fullness of man, his greatness and his joy?

If man only meets God in the world, if the world is the only place for this dialogue between God and man, if it is true that the

God of the Bible becomes only manifest in history—that is, in human actions, victories or defeats, exiles or revolutions—if the Word of God is always an act and if God calls men through the events that transform society, can one not say that God is wherever something new is born, wherever a new greatness is added to man—in scientific and technological discovery, in artistic creation and poetry, in the liberation of a people or a social revolution—wherever man becomes like unto the image of God, a creative being at every level of creation, economics, politics, and scientific, artistic or spiritual discovery? Is God not in everything that is not the mechanical continuation of the past, the mere result and product of the past, but that surpasses and fulfills the past all at once?

The work done to purify transcendence from all that makes it a mere remnant of primitive superstition leads to an interiorization of the lived experience of transcendence as "the attempt to transcend all human limitations with the help of God", according to the words of Carson Blake at the Ecumenical Congress of Heraclion. When this happens, transcendence becomes a dimension of every creative action of each of us. "Every conscience," wrote Bishop Robinson, "conceives the divine when it reflects on the operations by which it constitutes itself as such."

For a Marxist man is never the simple result or product of the past and the conditions of the present, but something different— and more, something which takes the past as a whole and surpasses it and its conditions. Could he not accept this concept of transcendence which then becomes a basic dimension of man and not only an attribute of God? He could call this moment of initiative and of "overcoming", in which Christianity has always seen the flowering and emergence of the divine in man's activity under the name of transcendence, a "dialectic" step forward.

Further Developments

Is it not the first task of the Church to discern "the signs of the times"—that is, the signs of God's presence and activity in the world—and to follow God there where he is?

Unbelievers perhaps expect that the Church should now "read" the world again, that she should judge men and political and social systems less by their attitude toward the Church than by their attitude toward man. Is it the Church's mission to defend the Church or to defend man? This is not an abstract or purely theoretical question but an immediately relevant and practical one.

Up until now it apears that the Church judged men, politics and governments according to their attitude toward the Church and the place they allotted to religion in the State. Nothing is said about Franco's crimes against man as long as he respects, or even increases, the Church's traditional privileges. The defense of the Church too often takes priority over the defense of man. This is so much the case that the Church is always on the side of those who defend her, even if this defense means crushing human beings, and always against those who fight her, even if this fight is necessary to set man free. Everything looks as if the Church were an end in herself and not a means of making hope visible.

When a high-ranking prelate extols the genocide in Vietnam, not a single official voice of the Vatican will unequivocally condemn him. It is said that this would not be according to tradition and the rules of diplomacy. But why should the Church not cease to be traditional and diplomatic and become prophetic for once? Why should she not say to those who turn a colonialist war into a crusade what the devout Abraham Lincoln said to some insolent priests: "Let us never say that God is on our side. Let us rather pray that we may be found on the side of God"?

It is not impossible that God is on the side of even those who deny him, or that it is precisely those persons who help to achieve God's revolution in the world. When God addressed himself to Cyrus, the king of the Persians, to accomplish his work, as related in Isaiah 45, he did not choose one of those who called themselves "servants of Yahweh". If we look beyond the parabolic and historical limits of this biblical narrative, may we not say that God revealed himself to man as that violent force which expresses itself in a social revolution or in a fight for national liberation? Is God not everywhere where a group of people struggles to make of each man a source of initiative and responsibility, a creator in the image of God?

It is therefore impossible to honor God in a Portugal that is in the grips of Fascist terror and where the last overtly colonialist war is being waged against Angola, even if the Virgin is honored in that regime. On the other hand, it is perhaps possible to honor God in Cuba where, within the space of three years, the exploitation of man, prostitution and illiteracy have been disposed of, which had been perpetuated throughout Latin America by centuries of colonial servitude and guaranteed by religion. There, perhaps, people struggle to make a man of each man, and so do God's business, even if a few Franco-minded priests are expelled.

Why should God always be on the side of the "establishment" and never on the side of change? Why should the Church not show more effectively that she has a prophetic mission, that she is capable of standing up to Mussolini or Hitler, even if this would entail martyrdom on a massive scale, and why should she reserve her excommunications for those who believe in the future and are prepared to risk themselves for it?

This conservative social attitude has always found strong support in the traditional interpretation of sin. Here again, Greek notions have played a large part in the transformation of biblical teaching. It looks very much as if the Christian notion of sin has been contaminated by that of the Greek *hubris* (excessive pride). Here two important aspects of Greek humanism have been lost. It is true that in Greek tragedy *hubris* brings about the ruin of the human being bold enough to brave the will of the gods, but it is a mark of the hero's greatness that he is willing to fight fate in a battle which he is bound to lose. Moreover, during the period when Greek civilization passed from one phase to another, the rebellious hero carried the torch for new values of the future, like Prometheus or Antigone. There, again, we can find greatness in the transgression. But in the traditional concept of sin the ideas of protest and revolt are central without having preserved the counterpart of the tragic grandeur of the revolt.

Pride is usually presented as the sin of sins. To sin is not to know one's place. This is how the biblical myth is interpreted. Sin is the transgression of an order which imposed prohibitions and restrictions on man: mental curiosity becomes a culpable spiritual concupiscence; the sexual blossoming of man becomes the concupiscence of the flesh; the inspiring passion to control nature and the human world becomes the temptation of Lucifer himself. Are there not political reasons behind this centuries-old assimilation of sin with insubordination, as the American theologian Harvey Cox has suggested?

When in the 4th century, with the rise of Constantine, Christianity became the dominant ideology and bestowed a religious guarantee on imperial authority and the social hierarchy of which it was the summit, and when for more than 1,000 years this formidable assimilation of the establishment with the order willed by God reigned supreme, sin became, in the words of Teilhard de Chardin, "an explanation of evil in a static concept of the world".

In such a perspective, the supreme sin, evil, became the disruption of this order. Parallel with this, piety implied the acceptance of this order. It is then hardly surprising that in the periods of great social upheaval—in the Renaissance or after the French Revolution—it was the rebel who was the most attractive hero, capable of stirring the heart and mind of man: Lucifer in Milton, Mephistopheles in Goethe, or Prometheus breaking his chains in Shelley.

During the 19th century every step forward toward human greatness started with a challenge to Christianity. Kierkegaard made the one true sin "the desperate refusal to be somebody". Marx taught that the social order is not a fixed and given reality but something man must achieve himself—hence, inevitably, the corollary that religion is the opium of the people. Nietzsche proclaimed that a God who does not allow man to be a creator deserved to be killed.

Thus, for over five centuries, since the time before the Renaissance and the disintegration of the feudal world, the divorce between man's striving after autonomy and the Church's traditional teaching grew wider and wider. Burckhardt has pointed out that medieval man was only aware of himself as part of a whole, as a segment of an order, a member of the community. The decisive turn in modern history came when the individual could think of himself as an autonomous reality, not outside his social relationships but, on the other hand, not merely the sum total or the result of those relationships. Has the Church been capable of taking this turn?

One may wonder whether the traditional notion of sin has not remained, to a certain degree, the metaphysical expression of the social order that dominated the West since Constantine and prevailed until the 15th century. Could one not understand the unifying principle of the various theological attempts made before and since Vatican Council II as the concern to bring about a new encounter between the Church and the world? If this is so, might the non-believer not expect the Church to rethink the notion of sin along these new lines and to interpret it in a way which accepts the spirit of our age?

The path has already been blazed by Teilhard de Chardin in his *Christologie et évolution.* Harvey Cox thinks that among Protestants, on the lines of Bonhoeffer, sin is less a matter of commission than of omission. According to him, sin, in the biblical tradition, is man's abdication, the refusal to accept responsibility. The real sin is that of Eichmann whose defense at his trial was invariably that he simply executed the orders of his Führer. Sin then is for me to be a mere puppet in an alienated society, controlled by the structures, accepting the stereotyped ways allotted to me from outside as guidance for my conduct, and allowing myself to be directed by the course of events. In short, sin is to want to be not *more* than man, but *less* than man.

One cannot really maintain here that the main theological and moral obstacle to such a dynamic and constructive reinterpretation of sin is that we must refuse violence. For here again our

view is warped by history if we can no longer see that to maintain the established order constitutes violence of a worse kind
than a revolt against such an order. To refuse an armed uprising
against Hitler's establishment was to aid and abet the worst kind
of violence—that of Auschwitz, Birkenau, Lidice and Oradour.

Of what physical and spiritual oppression of man did one become an accomplice when preaching passivity and non-violence
in the tsarist empire, that "prison of peoples", that soil of a
thousand years of oppression, pogroms and illiteracy? Of what
physical and spiritual cruelty does one become guilty today by
preaching passivity and non-violence in Latin America where, as
in India, hundreds of thousands die of hunger by the wayside in
the Andes and the regions of the Amazon?

We never have the choice between violence and non-violence,
but always between two kinds of violence, and no one can spare
us the concrete responsibility of deciding in each case which
violence is the least violent and the most fruitful for the blossoming of man. I repeat: to condemn the momentary violence of a
slave in revolt is to become the accomplice of the permanent and
silent violence of the one who keeps him in chains.

It is not a matter of "means" but of judging the "ends". Since
Constantine the Church has never proclaimed conscientious objection. If, then, she accepts that a Christian, and even a priest,
can carry arms and even take part in the violence of a national
war, in the name of what principle of "non-violence" can one
forbid anyone to take part in a social struggle or a revolution, unless one is prepared to condemn not the *means,* but the *ends?*

The Highest Vocation: Can It Be Achieved?

Historical conditions and the consequent delay in theological
development have led to the present situation, which is that Christians do not know how to live in a revolution. As to whether this
means that they lack a theology of revolution, it is not my task to
pronounce on this. However, there are precedents, as in Thomas
Münzer, or John Huss, or the English Levellers. The common

factor of these pioneers of the Christian revolution, or of a revolutionary Christianity, is perhaps that they took seriously the prayer which asks God that his will "be done *on earth* as it is in heaven".

Loisy said of the first generations of Christians that they expected the kingdom, but that it was the Church which came. In Münzer's militant millenarianism, Christians did not stop at an expectation of the kingdom, but proceeded to fight for it. "In its original essence," said Münzer, "faith gives us impossible things to do, of which delicate people cannot even imagine that they must come about." And here he stated the two essential themes of his theology of revolution: first, to apply the power of faith to the genuine transformation of this world in order to achieve the fullness of man, and second, never to forget to direct this renewal of life on earth to an always higher end. Here faith is no longer an opium but a ferment for the continuous creation of the world by man and an opening up of human history toward a horizon that knows no end.

If it is true that God has created each human being as a creator, is not the primary task of the Christian in this world to struggle against every form of alienation which degrades man by turning him from a subject into an object? This has a concrete meaning in our days. We must put an end to the proletarian condition which turns every worker not into an end, but into a *means*—a means to produce surplus value; an end to every form of colonialism or neo-colonialism which prevents millions of people from attaining the dignity of shaping their own destiny; an end to the arms race, cold war and actual war which force every nation to devote to the possible destruction of man the wealth and the power which would give millions of people the chance to achieve that properly human dignity, the chance to be cultured, responsible and creative.

The concrete struggle against those alienations of man (i.e., against everything that prevents millions of people from being human and creative in the likeness of God) can and must become the most powerful bond of solidarity between Christians and Marxists. Marxists should not forget what they owe, at this level, to Christian teaching.

Greek humanism discovered and elaborated an aspect and an essential "moment" of freedom: that of necessity and the knowledge of necessity. The highest freedom is then to have understood this necessity. But the idea of creation does not exist in the Greek concept of the world and of man. In the Judaeo-Christian concept, however, creation is primary and man's freedom is no longer defined as consciousness of necessity, but as a share in creative action. The story of the New Testament proclaims this Good News: man can, at any moment, begin a new future and control the laws of nature and society. Christ's resurrection is the exemplar of this new liberty: death itself—the final limit which marks our finiteness in such a ruthless manner—has been overcome.

This lived experience of the possibility to struggle free from a world that is "given" and to start a new future implies a double transcendence: the radical transcendence of God with regard to man, which is the basis of man's transcendence with regard to nature, to society and to his own history. If man is not the necessary product of the laws of nature and the structures of society, a mere prolonging of his past, he can only overcome the necessity of the world by sharing in the very act of the continuous creation of this world. It is up to the Marxists to recognize the importance of this Christian contribution in their heritage, not only from the cultural point of view but also from that of their militancy. But such a recognition gives them the right to expect a new dynamism from the Church.

In contrast with the first Adam who committed the major original sin of letting his conduct be dictated by an outside force and surrendering to the incitement of a serpent, Jesus, the second Adam, asserted man's essential prerogative by which he raised himself finally above the reign of nature. The essence of his message was to have shown that the forces which govern the world have no power to decide man's fate and that man can shake off every kind of dependence on any fate. Neither the forces of economics, nor class relations, nor the promptings of instinct and physiology, nor the psychological and moral pressures of family, class or nation, nor the structural demands of nature or society can wholly determine him, even if all these factors for a large part condition his actions and his thought.

Is not the essence of Jesus' message the proclamation of this transcendence, this dialectical "rising above", which frees man from the tyranny of infrapersonal or suprapersonal forces? When, then, will the Church remind us in her daily conduct that the demand which God has made known to us through Christ's "gesture" is to destroy the fatalism of history and the alienation of man? What unbelievers in this latter part of the 20th century expect of the Church first of all is that she restore to the message of Jesus this power to break the tyranny of the static, of what is given. This presupposes that a little less emphasis be put on personal piety and inward spirituality, and a little more on the historical and social dimension of love. Historically and traditionally the unbeliever often is given the impression that faith implies a withdrawal from the world, a withdrawal within oneself and within the sanctuary.

Is it true that there exists in life a special moment or place or activity, called "cult", to express man's response to God's invitation? Does the death of Christ, a scandal to all previous religions, not mean on the contrary a total solidarity with the world which excludes the possibility of marking off a particular domain for the sacred and of setting apart a special religious sector in life? But, then, if God's Word cannot be contained in a catechism or even a credal formula, if the Word of God is an act, in the very sense in which Jesus is the Word of God, how is the Church going to learn to read the deeds of God in the actions of man and in historical, political and social events?

Does this indispensable reading of the "signs of the times", in Pope John's words, not consist in trying to find out—humbly, that is, with the sole resources of a wholly human intelligence and without the pretense of transcending history, its groping, its errors and its failures—what kind of human relationships secure more fully for every man the chance to unfold his ability and his gifts to be a creator? Is this not the very heart of human hope, not outside life or outside history, but within this historical and carnal world where the pathetic dialogue between the human and the divine takes shape? Should the Church, then, not be on the side of all those, believers, unbelievers, heretics or atheists, who try to make this hope visible to man's eyes?

The concrete fulfillment of this task demands far more than individual charity or Church charity. It demands a basic redistribution of wealth and power, and this creates a basic doubt about what is usually called "the social doctrine of the Church". It is not enough to say, with Jaurès, that the Church only began to worry about the weak when they had become a force, or that the first "social encyclical", *Rerum Novarum,* came forty years after the Communist Manifesto, twenty-seven years after the first International, and above all, after the *Syllabus* and other prior documents that had anathematized for a century every political or social revolution.

However, instead of again opening up past wounds, it is more profitable to turn to the new dawn and to try to see more clearly what steps to take next in order to fill the gap which has developed between the Church and those who are in love with the future.

At the social level, the basic obstacle is that the "social doctrine of the Church" bases its attitude toward capitalism and socialism on the tragic postulate that "the right to private property does not derive from human laws but from nature; public authority cannot therefore abolish it" (*Rerum Novarum*). *Quadragesimo Anno* added: "Man has received the right to private property from nature, and *therefore from the creator.*" And Pius XII recalled that private property is "the guarantee of the essential freedom of the human person". Referring to *Rerum Novarum,* the encyclical *Mater et Magistra* underlines this: "Private ownership *even of productive goods* . . . is a natural right which the

State cannot suppress." The practical conclusion from this attitude was already clearly formulated in *Rerum Novarum:* "Hence it is clear that the basic principle, if one would undertake to alleviate the condition of the masses, must be the inviolability of private property. . . . The socialist theory of collective ownership is contrary to the natural rights of the individual."

On the basis of this principle the Church has never ceased to condemn the very essence of socialism while only condemning capitalism for its abuses. The question is whether this "principle" is a principle of theology or merely the survival of a political tradition which, since Constantine, constantly pretended to provide a theological justification for slavery and then for serfdom before it gave its support to the system of private ownership of the capitalist type and its corollary, the wage-system.

I do not intend to give a theological answer to this question, but I simply wish to point out that, on the straightforward level of history, private ownership of the means of production led capitalism to the worst excesses of cruelty and oppression of the individual, whether among workers in Europe or in the colonies. While it is true that private ownership, particularly of the means of production, gives the individual powerful weapons for his own expansion, it also leaves all those who do not have this ownership without defense against the tender mercies of this individualistic expansion. By its very principles, therefore, capitalism destroys that liberty which it claims to uphold.

Elementary logic, bloodily and historically confirmed by a century and a half of capitalist expansion, shows that if ownership is the guardian of freedom, the way to guarantee the freedom of all men (not only the privileged classes), and not to sacrifice the freedom of the vast majority of "have-nots" to a handful of privileged individuals who have, with this ownership of the means of production, an absolute dominion over the others, is to set up a collective ownership of the important means of production so that each can contribute his share of initiative and responsibility to the management of the economy in the production and distribution of the goods that are necessary for the full development of each and all.

This means that one of the next steps to take would be one which would correspond to what the vast masses of people, believers and unbelievers, would expect—namely, a change, at the social level, of the "social doctrine of the Church", a change which would lead her, in the light of a long historical experience and in the spirit of our age, no longer to condemn socialism in principle and capitalism only in its abuses, but capitalism in principle and socialism in its perversions.

It is true that the encyclical *Progressio Populorum* shows the beginning of a change with its more careful nuances. It subordinates "all rights, including that of ownership and free trade", to the first and basic human requirement, which is the promotion of every man and all men. It consequently declares that "private ownership is not an unconditional and absolute right of anyone".

But the practical conclusions remain timid. "A certain capitalism" is condemned, but not the principle of the whole system. Some have too hastily detected a revolutionary element in the sentence that "the common good sometimes demands expropriation". But expropriation for public use has nothing to do with socialism and is practiced by the most conservative governments. Revolution, however, is condemned "except in the case of obvious and prolonged oppression". Ultimately, "a certain capitalism", "the basic principle of liberalism as the rule for commercial exchange", is here called into question, but not the very principle of capitalism. It appears that a kind of State capitalism is acceptable; in any case, the principle of collective ownership of the means of production is not mentioned, nor is even the term "socialism". The previous "social" encyclicals, from *Rerum Novarum* on, are not only not repudiated but even referred to in the Preface as having correctly "shed the light of the Gospel on the social questions of their times".

But the new trend can no longer be reversed. Even if the official documents are but a weak reflection of the change that is taking place, man's thrust forward shows itself with increasing force. Moreover, if socialism has not been mentioned, it is at least not condemned—and this is undoubtedly progress, compared with the past.

Thus, after this encyclical on the development of the nations, and inspired by it to carry things further, a group of Third World bishops, from Latin America, Asia and Africa, led by the compulsive generosity of Archbishop Helder Camara of Brazil, have already drawn up a doctrinal outline for the Church of the near future. Sensitive to the anger of the nations where they live, they are anxious to dissociate their Church from a system of colonialist and capitalist oppression. They recall the solemn warning given by St. John in the Apocalypse to the Christians of that Rome which oppressed the nations and trafficked in slaves: "Leave, my people, leave that place lest, by your complicity in its errors, you have to suffer its wounds."

The bishops have declared in strong terms that the Church cannot identify herself with any political, economic or social system: "As soon as a system ceases to ensure what is good for the many to the advantage of the few, the Church must not only denounce the injustice but also dissociate herself from such an iniquitous system and be ready to cooperate with another system that is more just and better adapted to the needs of the age." If the abandonment of privileges is not accepted with good grace, "let us at least see the hand of God . . . in the events that impose this sacrifice upon us".

Speaking against those who have emigrated from revolutionary countries but who, under the pretext of religion, "in fact only fled in order to save their wealth and their privileges", the bishops add: "For over a century the Church has tolerated capitalism . . . hardly in accordance with the moral teaching of the prophets and the Gospel. She can only rejoice at seeing the dawn in mankind of another social system less remote from that moral teaching." Referring to "true socialism", they declare: "Far from resenting it, we should accept it gladly as a form of social life better suited to our times and more in conformity to the spirit of the Gospel. We shall then avoid that confusion of God and religion with the forces which oppress the world of the poor and the workers—namely, feudalism, capitalism and imperialism."

Discarding all ambiguity, the bishops' text recalls the declaration which Bishop Franic made at the Council: "Today the workers are more and more conscious of the fact that work constitutes a part of the human person. . . . Any buying or selling of work is a kind of slavery. . . . Human society is evolving in this direction, even in that system which we say is less sensitive to the human person than we are, Marxism."

In this document of the bishops of the Third World we may find the most advanced expression of the longing of those Christians who think that the Church's task in a world torn apart is to make hope visible.

Three Demands

In the chaos in which we try to think out ways and means of hoisting ourselves on to the level of that phenomenal change that is taking place in this 20th century, I offer a few reflections on what non-Christians expect the Church to do in the field of public morality, and these reflections can be reduced basically to three precise demands:

1. Recognition of the autonomy of human values in the fields of knowledge and action;

2. The embracing of man's Promethean ambition for a continuous creation of the world and of man by man;

3. A clear decision to enfranchise the word and the reality of *socialism* as the condition for the unbounded development of all men and the whole of man.

We are anxiously and hopefully waiting for this step to be taken because our common future depends on it. We do not ask any Christian to be less Christian but rather to be more fully Christian—that is, to contribute a Christian response to the problems of our time and in the spirit of our time. We are profoundly convinced of the fact that communism cannot fully succeed without integrating the best of the Christian contribution to the image of man. But this integration is only fully possible if the basic Christian values are no longer obscured by the conservative attitude of the Church.

Christoph Wagner/*Neuss, W. Germany*

Social Cybernetics as a Permanent Function of the Church

The opening up of the Church to the world, implicit in the Church's mission, demanded by the developments of the modern age and explicitly affirmed and proclaimed as a program by Vatican Council II, has led to a heightened, almost excessive, awareness of problems in the Christian's mind. And yet this awareness of problems is not matched by any faculty in the Church for solving these problems. For this reason, awareness of problems turns into criticism, not only from without, but from within.

Awareness of problems, unsupported by the possibility of solving them, leads to unrest, to impatience with the tempo of change in the Church and to psychological frustration. Thus a false antithesis between conservative and progressive could arise, threatening to be confirmed by an actual disruptive development. In order to avoid this, it is urgently required that we create a new equilibrium between the burden of problems and the Church's capacity to solve them. Thus the expectations of the People of God can be fulfilled. In this article we will discuss ways to achieve this goal.[1]

---

[1] I have never seen a systematic treatment of social cybernetics that went further than a discussion of the relation of man to machine. I owe my ideas, therefore, to men rather than to books: Peter Brückner (Han-

Guiding as a Method of Solving the Problems

Since her origin, the Church has quite frankly used many methods of guiding in the solving of her problems. During the past two centuries of industrialization, however, because the necessity of guiding became more universal, its methods more diverse and its machinery the object of new scientific disciplines, the Church has largely lost sight of the possibilities of guiding.

What is guiding? The answer is better given by an example than by a definition. First of all, the traveler decides on his destination; let us say he is driving to Rome. Then he decides on his *itinerary,* the roads he will take, where he will stop. For example, he decides to cross the Brenner Pass. Only then does he begin to steer. On account of all sorts of accidental alterations along his route—road construction and so on—as a rule he is constantly compelled to *adapt his itinerary*—i.e., in order to attain his goal, he will constantly have to alter separate sectors of his route.

The surroundings include not just (1) the external route, but also (2) the (man-made) motor vehicle—for which reason the apparently uncomplicated process of driving straight ahead is liable to constant adaptation—and (3) the other drivers on the road, whose behavior is much less predicable than his own. Consequently, the complexity of traveling in heavy traffic makes defensive driving necessary; it presupposes a prognostication of the behavior of the human environment.

In the example we have taken the driver fulfills three functions simultaneously—hence the severe physical strain upon all car drivers—which, in the classic analogy of cybernetics, namely, a sea journey, correspond to three vocations: the captain is responsible for arriving at the destination, the pilot for the adaptation of the itinerary to the current environment, and the helms-

over); Paulus Engelhardt (Walberberg); Hans Georg Gadamer (Heidelberg); Wilhelm Korff (Bonn); Klaus Lefringhausen (Velbert); Klaus Meyer zu Utrup (Ebingen); H. K. Schuff (Dortmund); Rudolf Warnke (Beuel bei Bonn).

man for the transmission of the itinerary to the ship's steering mechanism.[1a]

This example clearly shows what has happened during the past 160 years of industrialization. Following the delegation of human effort to machines (mechanization) and its recoordination with the working man (rationalization), guiding operations (automation) and, more recently, the function of the pilot have been transferred to machines (automation in the strict sense). The computer takes over from the pilot; only the captain's function of deciding on the destination remains incapable of delegation. By this progressive increase in guiding, man becomes progressively liberated so that he is free to devote himself to ever new possibilities of guiding.

In this way a new discipline arose: cybernetics. It is of little importance how one defines cybernetics: as the *art* of increasing efficiency, as a superordinate *science* of all the techniques of guiding, or even as the *mode of thought* appropriate to solving the problem. The high degree of abstraction about cybernetics would permit the following definition: it is the transformation of a *status quo* in the direction of a set goal (target) in terms of an adaptable program, by means of constant *feed back* of *status-quo* information to the programmer.[2]

Anyone who increases the efficiency of an action eliminates sources of error and minimizes risk; anyone who has to realize ideas or alter unsatisfactory conditions has to think cybernetically if he is not to fail in his duty.

Guiding Techniques in the Social Sphere

One of the most remarkable phenomena of recent days is the application of cybernetic thinking to social reality, with a view to changing it. The simplest demonstration of this fact is

---

[1a] The metaphor of the helmsman was one of Plato's favorites. I do not know which of his dialogues gave Norbert Wiener the idea of using it as a concept of the science of guiding and controlling. Cf. Norbert Wiener, *Cybernetics* (New York, 1948).

[2] The high degree of abstraction and the universality of cybernetics are best reflected in the omnibus volumes VI–VII of the *Enzyklopädie des Atomzeitalters* (Geneva, 1959).

the transference of the language of engineering to the realm of social behavior. Advertising is defined as "creation of demand", public relations as "engineering of consent", a political election campaign as "making a president"—and these are but examples from a host of techniques already being practiced in the human sphere. In totality they are described as "human engineering".[3]

It is highly significant, however, that this penetration of technological thinking into the social sphere has to do neither with usurpation nor with luxury, and only in exceptional cases has it to do with aberrations. It is demanded by the need for pragmatic answers to basic necessities. Critics as well as advocates of industrial society seem to have ignored the fact that every liberation of man from the task of guiding, through its delegation to a machine, relentlessly creates social problems, which in turn are so grave and urgent that they can only be overcome by calling in processes of social guiding.

Here are a few examples. The changeover to mass production by conveyor-belt processes demanded a whole host of human techniques in order to ensure, to some extent synthetically, cooperation and contentment among the labor force. Having satisfied initial needs, it became urgently necessary to increase demand by advertising in order to keep open the jobs which had been created. When a person is precipitated into a huge office, or when computers are introduced, a special educational program is absolutely necessary in order to ensure the individuality of those affected.

Automation itself is still the best example. The labor which this liberates must speedily be diverted into a new sphere as yet unaffected by automation—today found mostly in the office sector. Should there be even slight delay, social unrest will almost certainly result.

If this is true, there is no human alternative to taking over guiding techniques in the human sphere. Moreover, from the

[3] The first omnibus volume on the problem of human engineering, by Heidelberg scholars, is in preparation. Practical methods of group work according to the Socratic principle have been developed by R. and H. Hauser, *The Fraternal Society* (London, 1962).

anthropological viewpoint, the capacity to be guided could presumably be regarded as man's specific differential. Man's dignity cannot permanently be defended by those who wish to limit his most characteristic faculty or obstruct its application to man himself.

Thus the problem is turned around the other way; it is not the trespass of guiding into the social sphere that is to be deplored, but the insufficiency of the present solutions of the problems by means of social guiding.

The much-quoted view that man's mind is limping along behind technology is basically true. Mind and society also have to be guided so that the inhuman subservience of man to an environment of apparatus and automatons, which he himself has created, is ended and gives way to a sharing of work between man and machines, wherein man will be more than just a source of error.

Organization of Structure and Process as Methods of Social Guiding

Social systems—by which we mean more than accidental groupings of men—display at least two kinds of organization: of structure—analogous to the vascular system—and of process —analogous to the circulation of the blood. The two must be interdependent if social life is to be possible and if an exchange of information and activities is to be guaranteed.[4]

Accordingly, social guiding can make use of two levers: by founding, supporting, or dissolving institutions, it can change the structural organization; by sending, receiving and reporting back information, it can change the organization of processes. Processes of communication, however, are dependent upon the structural organization; by institutionalization, therefore, greater social changes can be achieved than by information. If, for example, we regard the Church as a social system, sheer infor-

[4] Information on the connection between organization and communication is provided in *Kommunikation im Industriebetrieb* by Joachim Hermann and Wolfgang Zapf (Frankfurt, 1955).

mation (preaching) will require a structural organization (the Church), but on the other hand the structural organization will have to be tested to see whether and how far it helps or hinders the realization of the aim of giving information.

There are few opportunities for structural change—revolution, change of government, change in constitution—for every social system possesses a collective egoism with self-preservation for its aim. Consequently, guided information is the method of adaptation to lesser changes in environment, whereby a psychical change of attitude in those affected suffices, and a change of system is not necessary. Such a change always comes about in two stages: first by winning over a multiplicator group of active opinion-forming people (e.g., the college of the apostles), and then by winning over a larger body of adherents. As a rule, two other groups are left behind: the uncommitted and the uninformed.[5]

Both methods of social guiding are based upon the assumption that the consent of the people affected is essential. Obviously the alternative of coercion is possible: overthrow of institutions through propaganda in the form of the issuing of one-sided, monopolized information, with no basic reference to feedback, although modern dictatorships devise their own methods of creating and controlling consent. There is also the possibility of chance guiding.

Manipulation and the Fear of Manipulation as an Unsolved Problem Facing the Transition to a Guided Society

Scarcely any other ethical problem arouses so much public interest today, both in East and West, as that concerning the

[5] A survey of the pattern of means of communication is found in Karl Steinbach, *Die informierte Gesellschaft* (Stuttgart, 1966). To what extent this is sound enough to be the basic model for the study of sociological communications is explained by Gerhard Maletzke, *Psychologie der Massenkommunikation* (Hamburg, 1963). On the effects of social communication, cf. Wilbur Schramm (editor), *Grundfragen der Kommunikationsforschung* (Munich, 1964).

manipulation of men by men through the quiet bypassing of explicit, voluntary consent. The vague concept of manipulation is met by the vague sense of uneasiness. For this very reason it is extremely liable to become loaded with negative associations. The heart of this fear is the thought that manipulated man will be reduced to a mere means to an end, whereas his dignity as an end in himself ought to be safeguarded.

It must be admitted in the first place that distrust of manipulation is well founded, for we cannot shut our eyes to bad forms of social guiding. Public discussion then centers around these aberrations. Subliminal advertising, the mass persuasion of housewives on their own doorsteps and tendentious political propaganda all fall under real criticism. But this criticism also leads us to neglect the necessity of a genuine psychological industry.[6] The way in which the average man reacts to these human engineers and their aberrations will now be attested by a few consonant results of many market, opinion and motive research studies.

The Dogma of One's Own Rationality and Imperviousness to Persuasion

The average newspaper reader, when asked about his personal attitude to politics, will quote ideas from his morning paper. When invited to criticize the paper, he will, on the other hand, slip into the role of critic and produce arguments against this point of view. In both cases he will pretend to document his own opinion. Likewise, the housewife pretends to justify every purchase on rational grounds, even when she has demonstrably been induced to buy through advertisement, all the while declaring that she is impervious to such influence. As a result advertisement not only redescribes goods so that they seem more personal

[6] The writings of Vance Packard (*The Hidden Persuaders*, etc.) add up to a polemical criticism of the manipulated society. Hans Magnus Enzenberger reflects on the topic "Bewusstseinsindustrie" in *Einzelheiten* I (Frankfurt, 1962). A historical contribution is provided by Christoff Neumeister, *Grundsätze der forensischen Rhetorik* (Munich, 1964).

(a dishwashing machine becomes a domestic servant), but alters the rational explanation of the act of purchasing.[7]

The Exclusiveness of Individual Thinking

Buyers and sellers, shareholders, electors, Church attenders—whatever roles men may play, they feel that they are individuals and resist any diminution of this sense of their own value. The conditioning of the individual by the group (cf. the milieu-pressure to which Churchgoers could be subjected) remains hidden to them because they do not want to become aware of it. A result of this erroneous estimation, again in the field of advertising, is that an explanation of the true collective character of the supply of goods and services would be too expensive. Instead of this, individuality is sold as a psychological bonus along with mass produced goods.

The Myth of the Possibility of Pure Information

The view is widespread, even in intellectual spheres, that there *is* such a thing as a report without commentary, a purely factual story without any interpretation, and hence pure information. We are not thinking of the fundamental interest involvement of all social communications. Accordingly, suspicion is cast upon information supplied by an interested party if it is not corroborated by the other side (e.g., Church announcements from the pulpit that are not repeated on television).

In this we are leaving completely out of consideration the reciprocal effect between, for example, the editorial staff and the readership, which can lead to the editors adapting themselves to the readers, so that the readers are no longer presented with information that does not harmonize with their most obvious

[7] Consumer advertising and engineering the commodity market are described by Willi Bongard, *Fetische des Konsums* (Hamburg, 1964); Peter Brückner, *Die informierende Funktion der Wirtschaftswerbung* (Berlin, 1967); Reinhold Bergler, *Psychologie des Marken—und Firmenbildes* (Göttingen, 1963); Wilhelm Dreier, *Funktion und Ethos der Konsumwerbung* (Münster, 1965).

need for information. It is precisely at this point that the greatest consequences for salesmanship arise. It is interesting, further, that the old professions concerned with molding public opinion (lawyers, teachers, clergy) and the old institutions (schools, governments) come less (and later) under the fire of criticism than do the new professions and techniques. In the case of the pre-technical guiding processes, we see with special clarity the exonerating effect of custom.

The true aims, techniques and possibilities of steering in the social field remain unknown for the very reason that the fear of manipulation prevents their becoming known. The actual capacity of our fellowmen to be influenced and manipulated is increased by this very thing. There is, therefore, a need for de-mythologizing and deideologizing the so-called facts of opinion, in order first of all to break out of this vicious circle of self-inflicted immaturity.

When this is accomplished one is astonished to discover how far the various human techniques have already advanced toward becoming an impressive integrated system of guided opinion-formation and attitude-changing. Once again the world of advertising supplies an example. Competition stands at the origin of advertising. Notwithstanding, without prejudice to competition, the high total cost of advertising, matched by no comparable expenditure upon opinion-formation of any other style, led to a stabilization of the competitive society. Rival advertising measures complement one another to become one colossal communal advertisement for the principle of consumption.

At the moment, however, commercial advertising is close to becoming a closed system in which not only consumers' desires, but all desires, receive an offer of satisfaction. On the other hand, however, things that are fundamentally novel have found it difficult to make any impact. This explains the successful usurpation of transcendental motifs—i.e., motifs that point far beyond the horizon of the consumption process (e.g., life insurance that promises "life after death" in the remembrance of one's family, or manufacturers of detergents who offer a "good conscience" as a bonus in addition to care of linen).

The economic temptation is never far away to avoid an expensive change of mentality and instead to provide the existent mentality with pseudo contents, thus making a short-term adaptation to circumstances.[8] It would be more correct to yield to the necessity of universal guiding. Hitherto only State socialism has attempted this, although this does not imply that the State ought to be the sole guiding agency.

Social Cybernetics as the Missing Science of the Non-Coercive Steering of Social Changes

Taking the fear of manipulation and also the aberrations of social guiding seriously, many are led to the false conclusion that we have here an ethical problem capable of immediate solution. An ethics of rejection of manipulation, however, would be no more than a sheer reflection of the demoscopic *status quo:* it would indeed express the *vis inertiae* of society, but not its orientation toward the future. The problems of social steering first demand scientific, and only then ethical, mastery. First of all, the phenomena must be isolated; only then ought they to be called to judgment. In other words, what is missing is a science of the guiding of social change that is more than the existent theories and techniques of social change.

The chief task of such social cybernetics will be to seek ways of achieving the necessary adaptation of mind and of social forms to environmental changes in an unbloody fashion. It will have to develop processes of guiding that lie between the extremes of force and the autonomy of chance.

In the United States the sciences dealing with man have already been reorganized as the behavioral sciences and thus have proclaimed their affinity with natural science. However, this should not conceal the fact that there are specific laws govern-

[8] Cf. the analysis of the world of pseudo-realities by Daniel J. Boorstin, *Das Image* (Hamburg, 1964).

ing the study and change of social systems. One or two distinctions may clarify this point.

1. The production of data about men by men is more difficult on account of subjectivity on both sides (cf. the problems of opinion research by demoscopes wherein the investigator appears as a source of error). The one interrogated can never give a factually correct answer about himself, but basically he already interprets the expectations of the interrogator into his answer.[9]

2. Over a very recent period we have gathered so few data about man collectively that we can find no probabilities as high as are to be found in the natural sciences. Obviously, greater uncertainty also lies in the spontaneity of human beings who, because of their fundamental openness to their environment, are able to show behavior that deviates from the norm far more easily than do other forms of life.

3. The publication of data or prognoses inevitably produces a reaction in the social field. For example, an electoral forecast will influence the undecided. The publication of a timetable will either encourage or discourage the builders of aircraft to produce planes, and so either confirm or refute the validity of the prognosis.

4. On account of the comparatively low determinability of human behavior, the category of causality very rarely possesses the widespread importance it possesses in the non-human realm (e.g., attraction-reflex reaction). In contrast, the basic cybernetic category of feedback assumes central importance.[10]

Indeed, within the social sphere everything is reciprocally connected to everything else (the sympathy doctrine of the neo-Platonists postulated this as a cosmic principle). And so the relation between social systems based upon feedback is much more difficult to analyze or to influence than that between rigidly programmed systems, machines or lower forms of life.

[9] Cf. E. Noelle-Neumann, *Umfragen in der Massengesellschaft* (Hamburg, 1963), pp. 32ff.
[10] On the concept of feedback, cf. Stafford Beer, *Cybernetics and Management* (London, 1959), chapter 4.

Any future social cybernetics will have to distinguish clearly between *things as they are* and *things as they ought to be,* between programs and goals of the current social system. In this way two things may arise. There might be a rehabilitation of Utopia, for every social system requires a goal higher than the immanent goal of its own survival. The setting of a goal will always have a utopian character as long as its attainability is not proved. A realizable Utopia, however, can immediately become a program.[11]

Presumably the problem of positivism will turn up again if, by analogy to the processes of technology, a continuous feedback begins between sociological analysis of things as they are and social programs. Such programs presuppose the setting of goals, and these in turn presuppose assessments. Only those who remain stuck at analysis can refuse to make assessments.

Social cybernetics, like technology and economics, will constantly seek to contrive the end-means relation in such a way that the smallest outlay will bring the largest yield or that a constant outlay will bring an ever increasing yield. Only to that extent may we entertain any hopes of an unbloody revolution.

Here, then, is where a direct encounter could take place between technical-economic and social thinking. Only when this encounter has taken place will the new starting points of a cybernetic social ethics become evident. There are one or two questions which may now be anticipated—for example, the question whether a particular social system is worth stabilizing or ought to be superseded by new structures. Above all, however, the goal-setting of a social system will always remain an ethical, and never a technical, question. The same holds true of the fixation of the secondary conditions which ought to remain unaffected by the steering procedures.

The doctrine of freedom, as we have hitherto known it, can be understood as advocacy of maximum personal scope for action through minimum guiding. If this assumption becomes obsolete, freedom must be thought about again. In the process, one

[11] Georg Picht, *Prognose, Utopie, Planung* (Stuttgart, 1967).

or two Marxist arguments will certainly prove worthy of discussion.

Theology and Social Changes in the Mind of the Church

Those who are active in the service of the Church often say that theology is much too abstract to be of any help to them. This is true. Although by adopting dialectic methods and empirical social study theology has put itself in a position where it is better fitted than formerly to describe the dynamic of the surrounding world and the dynamic of the Church that is its compelling consequence, what is still completely lacking is the preparation of ecclesiastical decisions and actions in regard to steering by means of the techniques of prognosis, planning, etc.[12] As a result, theology presents more or less relevant analyses of *things as they are* and more or less realizable ideas of *what ought to be,* but without arriving at any clear alternatives for the Church's strategy.

This failure to produce a strategy is most clearly seen if we look at the contradictory statements about the *leit-motif* of Vatican Council II—*aggiornamento.* Adaptation is not only a concept for group-sociological analysis, but, on the higher plane of abstraction, one of the most important of all cybernetic concepts. The adaptation of the social system that is the Catholic Church to the changes in her own system, and the relation of that system to the surrounding world, can be analyzed and mastered in no other way than by the acceptance of cybernetic principles into the *instrumentarium* of the Church. Even those ideas about pastoral planning that have already taken root here and there presuppose this acceptance.

The alternative of passive reaction upon the surrounding world would be tantamount to waiting for the atrophy of more functions. The alternative provided by a Church predominantly in-

---

[12] The first drafts of a Church cybernetics are found in Klaus Meyer zu Utrup, "Die Bedeutung des Alten Testaments für eine Transformation der Kirche heute," in *Theologische Existenz heute* 135 (Munich, 1966); Jürgen Seetzen, "Entwicklung zu einer allgemein Systemtechnik," in *Pastoraltheologie* 56 (Göttingen).

tent upon conserving what is left of her present social system would be bound to end in the collapse of sheer passivity in face of the changes going on in the Church's own system. The risk of adaptation cannot be avoided (by conservatism) but only minimized (by guiding). This task of minimizing the risk falls to theology.

Conclusions

1. In order to be able to fulfill her function in the future, the Church will have to become dynamically synchronized with society, engaging in a constant exchange of information and activity with society. Only in this way will she be able to exert her specific effect as the salt and the yeast of society.

2. The Church will have to functionalize her structural organization. In the process it may become necessary to amend the exclusiveness of the hierarchical guiding principle.

3. The Church will hardly be able to fulfill her ministry to society without organizing that function efficiently—avoiding, of course, the danger of changing that ministry into a mere service. The twofold stringency affecting the Church forces her to do this: the shortness of time left to accomplish certain social changes, and the meager supply of effective apostolic agencies.

4. The service society most requires is the presentation of goals beyond the collective egoism of social part-systems. It is true that revelation has provided the Church with fundamental goals, but tradition alone is unable to tell us how to develop these goals for the society of tomorrow. This can be done only through the constant feedback of secular information into the traditional program of the Church.

5. The Church will always be faced with the task of determining the secondary conditions of social guiding as the secondary conditions of humanity.[13]

[13] For further information on this topic, cf. Klemens Brockmöller, *Industriekultur und Religion* (Frankfurt, 1964); Peter Brückner, *Freiheit, Gleichheit, Sicherheit—Von den Widersprüchen des Wohlstands* (Frankfurt, 1966); Jean Fourastié, *Die grosse Hoffnung des 20. Jahrhunderts* (Cologne, ³1954); *ibid., Die grosse Metamorphose des 20. Jahrhunderts*

Because human society is dynamic, in the end no one can know what being human means. A static concept of humanity is of no use to us. The concept of humanity has constantly to be sought afresh. From time to time the Church will be able to humanize the secular techniques of guiding, but only if she herself is aware of the possibilities of that guiding—i.e., if she succeeds in recognizing guiding as her own commission to service. Does not St. Paul himself list cybernetics among the gifts of the Spirit that should unfold within the Church (1 Cor. 12, 28)?

(Düsseldorf, 1964); Arnold Gehlen, *Anthropologische Forschung* (Hamburg, [3]1964); *ibid., Die Seele im technischen Zeitalter* (Hamburg, [4]1961); Vance Packard, *The Naked Society* (London, 1964); Lübbe, Karus, Angerer, Lohff, and Moltmann, *Modelle der Gesellschaft von morgen* (Göttingen, 1966); Paulus Engelhardt, "Der Mensch und seine Zukunft," in *Festschrift für Max Muller* (Freiburg/Munich 1966); Hans Georg Gadamer, "Notes on Planning for the Future," in *Daedalus* (Spring, 1966).

Aldo Ferrer/*Buenos Aires, Argentina*

World Trade and International Cooperation for Development

I

TECHNICAL PROGRESS AND THE INTERDEPENDENCE OF NATIONS THROUGH TRADE

Trade is historically the most important channel of interdependence between nations. Since the end of World War II, trade, as a result of this interdependence, has grown rapidly. But the underdeveloped countries have largely been left out of this process of growth, and their share of world trade has suffered a noticeable decline. In 1950 the underdeveloped countries contributed 32% of world exports; by 1962 this share had dropped to 21%. During the same period the exports of developed countries with a market economy increased from 60% to 66% of world exports, and those of countries with a controlled economy from 8% to 13%.[1]

The principal cause of this relative decline in the exports of underdeveloped countries is the fact that most of their products are foodstuffs and raw materials, and the demand for these categories has increased very slowly. In fact, in 1961 90% of the products of the underdeveloped countries was in raw materials, and the increase in these between 1955 and 1961 was only 2.2% per year. World exports of manufactured goods, on the other hand, of which the underdeveloped countries con-

[1] UNCTAD, *Analysis of the Trends of World Trade* (New York, 1964).

61

tributed only 4%, increased by 8.7% during the same period. The period 1955–1961 is generally taken as a fair index of long-term trends.[2]

The reasons for the slow growth in exports of primary products from the underdeveloped countries have been extensively examined in recent literature on economic development. They include factors such as the low-revenue elasticity of the demand for foodstuffs, the replacement of raw materials such as wool, cotton, rubber and leather by synthetic products, the decline in the overall proportion of raw materials to manufactured products due to increased productivity brought about by technological progress, and the substitution of certain materials for others (such as the growing use of aluminium in place of other metals). All these have affected the exports of various products from the underdeveloped countries.

These factors are all due to technical progress and the changing patterns of demand that result from an overall increase in the volume of world trade. However, they have been reinforced by the protectionist policies adopted by the industrialized countries to defend and promote their own production of foodstuffs and raw materials. This factor in its turn has naturally diminished their demand for imports of raw materials from the underdeveloped countries. Furthermore, the developed countries have registered rapid advances in the field of their own primary produce (agriculture for example), thereby not only being able to satisfy a greater proportion of their home demand but even to increase their exports of these same commodities. And so we have the paradoxical fact that the rate of expansion of primary products from the developed countries with a market economy was more than double that of the underdeveloped countries: 5.2% against 2.2%, comparing the same products over the years 1955–1961. And if petroleum is excluded, the imbalance in the figures becomes even more marked—5.2% against 0.8%.[3]

Trade in manufactured goods shows the same imbalance be-

[2] Ibid.
[3] Ibid.

tween rates of expansion in industrialized countries and under-developed countries. This is because the latter depend mainly on simple manufacturing processes, such as textiles, while the predominant categories of exports from the industrialized countries are the products of engineering and chemicals, which have a faster rate of growth.

These tendencies show clearly enough that world trade is increasingly concentrated in countries with developed market economies or controlled economies. In 1961 these were responsible for 96% of the world's exports of manufactured goods and 64% of its primary produce. These proportions show an increase over 1955, and though the time span is short, it can be taken as a reliable indication of longterm trends.

What has happened is that the countries specializing in primary produce and the industrialized countries are no longer complementary to each other on the economic plane. This type of world division of labor had predominated in the world economy from the middle of the 19th century up to the great depression of 1930. Under present conditions, on the other hand, "the degree of 'complementariness' is greater between countries with highly diversified industrial structures. Extreme differentiation of products and manufacturing processes creates certain commercial possibilities for products statistically classified in the same group; this class of 'complementariness' has been defined as 'intraindustrial specialization'. It is in the field of highly diversified industrial structures that the changes and innovations which widen the commercial ambit are found".[4]

These tendencies in world trade have a profound effect on the capacity of the underdeveloped countries to develop, and on their ability to share in the fruits of modern technical progress. Under the conditions existing before 1930, world trade allowed countries which specialized in primary production to have a certain share of the benefits of technical progress, although this was largely concentrated in the spheres of agriculture and raw ma-

[4] UNCTAD, *Study of World Trade and Development* (New York, 1966).

terials and complementary activities. Then came the crisis of world trade in the 1930's, followed by the isolationism provoked by World War II. When, after 1945, world trade resumed its role of transmitter of technical progress and promoter of interdependence between nations, the underdeveloped countries found themselves left on the sidelines of the process and world trade became an activity increasingly confined to the developed countries.

The principal problem of this last third of the 20th century is generally admitted to be how to overcome the intolerably low standard of living of two-thirds of the human race. This means that the lagging trade of those countries must be analyzed in the wider context of international cooperation designed to overcome the problem of underdevelopment and to achieve a more equitable state of affairs in which the whole of humanity will be able to share in and benefit from the fruits of technical and scientific progress; in the developed countries this progress has already led to high standards of living and to a creative approach to all aspects of personal life and social activity.

The recent encyclical *Populorum progressio* analyzed, among other things, the meaning of this international cooperation to overcome underdevelopment, and I think it provides an excellent frame of reference, enabling us to treat the problems of external trade of the developing countries in the wider context of relations between developed and underdeveloped countries. I propose, therefore, to examine those parts of the encyclical that deal with international cooperation for development, including the problems of the external trade of underdeveloped countries.

II

The Encyclical and the Problem of Underdevelopment

The first thing that must be done is to stress the importance given in the encyclical to the necessity of remedying the economic and social conditions of the underdeveloped countries. It states that "today the most important fact, of which everyone should take notice, is that the social question has taken on a worldwide dimension" (n. 3). It adds that "development is the new name for peace" because "excessive economic, social and cultural differences between peoples provoke tensions and discords and endanger peace" (n. 76). Therefore, "everyone [should] be deeply convinced of this: what is at stake is the life of the poor nations, civil peace in those countries in the process of development, and the peace of the world" (n. 55).

Paul VI underlines the fact that two-thirds of humanity live in intolerable conditions, and he stresses the threat to world peace posed by this fact. Most observers of the international scene would agree in correlating both internal and international disturbances of peace with the tensions resulting from underdevelopment. The urgency of the pope's message can be realized when one takes into account the fact that, for the first time in history, the powerful nations can no longer settle their differences by having recourse to the final resort of armed confrontation. The destructive power of nuclear weapons prevents them from going to war to settle their differences without endangering the very survival of the whole human race.

Yet at the same time, and also for the first time in history, we have the resources to eliminate, completely and in a relatively short space of time, hunger, illiteracy and all the other scourges that degrade the human condition. The productive capacity implicit in the level reached by modern science and technology, together with the resources available throughout the world, would make it possible to launch a massive program of economic expansion that would result in a rapid increase in food production, industrial output and the availability of services essential to health and education. I shall attempt to detail these possibilities later in this article.

The encyclical proposes a series of measures that should be adopted both by underdeveloped countries and the whole international community. "The peoples themselves have the prime responsibility to work for their own development. But they will not bring this about in isolation. Regional agreements among weak nations for mutual support, understandings of wider scope entered into for their help, more far-reaching agreements to establish programs for closer cooperation among groups of nations —these are the milestones on the road to development that leads to peace" (n. 77).

The proposals in the encyclical are very important for an analysis of international cooperation for development. They are directly applicable and reflect the recent findings of theories of economic development and the data collected since the end of World War II on this subject. They cover two main aspects: a program of concrete measures to be taken and the principles to be respected while putting these measures into effect.

III

A PROGRAM OF INTERNATIONAL COOPERATION FOR DEVELOPMENT

The concrete measures suggested cover the following points: creation of a great "World Fund" to finance development; conditions governing loans for development; economic cooperation between neighboring countries; commercial policies in international trade. I propose to make a brief analysis of each of these.

1. *Creation of a Great "World Fund"*

The encyclical proposes that this fund should be financed by a part of the money now devoted to military expenditures "in order to relieve the most destitute", and it adds: "What is true of the immediate struggle against want, holds good also when there is a question of development. Only worldwide collaboration, of which a common fund would be both a means and a symbol, will succeed in overcoming vain rivalries and in establishing a fruitful and peaceful exchange between peoples" (n. 51).

It would be no exaggeration to say that this proposal is the pivotal point around which the encyclical's whole program of international cooperation revolves. The scope of the matter is important: a United Nations report estimated that total world expenditures on armaments and defense had reached the sum of $120,000,000,000 in 1961. This figure equalled the total world exports of goods in the same year and was half the total world accumulation of capital. Despite the fact that similar estimates have not been made for more recent years it is obvious, in view of the increasing world tension since then, that overall defense costs must have increased and, at the very least, maintained the same relationship to the other figures.[5]

In contrast to world expenditures on armaments and defense—confined almost entirely to industrialized countries, principally the United States and the Soviet Union—we have the figure of $6,600,000,000 as the figure for the net flow of official financial resources from the industrialized countries, including those of Eastern Europe, to the developing countries and international credit institutions—in other words, a little more than 5% of the figure for defense.[6]

A good idea of the relative importance of defense expenditures and development aid can be gained from relating these sums to the gross national products of the industrialized countries. (I shall have to exclude those of Eastern Europe for which no figures are available.) In the United States, Western Europe, Canada and Japan, defense and armament expenditures amounted to about 8% of the gross national product, while official development aid amounted to less than 1%, and this latter figure has been decreasing in recent years. In 1961 it was 0.65%; in 1966 it had fallen to 0.5%.[7] Seen from the other end, the amount that developing countries receive in aid amounts to about three dollars per person per year and represents less than 2% of their gross national product. This is clearly a very small contribution to a significant increase in growth rate.

[5] United Nations, *Economic and Social Consequences of Disarmament* (New York, 1962).
[6] World Bank, *Annual Report, 1965–66* (Washington, D.C., 1966).
[7] Ibid.

Therefore, the observation contained in a recent report of the World Bank is justified: "Means to stimulate economic growth of the less developed countries have an important place among the declared objectives of almost all the industrial nations. . . . However, in many cases there is a considerable difference between the principles they declare and what they do in practice." [8]

It is interesting to see what would happen if Paul VI's proposal to create a world fund, made up of part of the money spent on arms were actually adopted. If the international community were to devote $120,000,000,000 a year (the sum spent on defense and armaments in 1961) to collaboration in aiding the underdeveloped countries for ten years, really remarkable results would be achieved. Working on basic economic relationships,[9] it seems likely that the population of the underdeveloped world will increase from its present 2,400,000,000 to 3,070,000,000 by 1977, and that the average per capita income could in the same period increase from $150 to $450 if aid were forthcoming on this scale. This is an average increase of over 10% per year.

At this level of average income, given reasonably equitable distribution, hunger and most of the other scourges that accompany underdevelopment would be eliminated. If, after this ten-year period, international aid still continued on the same scale, a period of general prosperity in every country on the planet would be ushered in by the end of this century. Those countries that are underdeveloped at present would have reached an economic level at which they could ensure their own continued growth. The amount the developed countries would have contributed to this undertaking in the last third of the century, allowing for a proportional increase in the amount corresponding to the expansion of their own economies, would have

[8] Ibid., p. 26.

[9] It is supposed that the receiving nations have a capital-product ratio of 2:1 and a constant net capitalization of 8.3% of the gross national product. Population growth is 2.5% per year.

amounted to about 3% of the cumulative gross product over the period.

These calculations are of course exclusively theoretical. Their practical viability depends on the international political situation, and this seems to be moving further and further away from a rational, realistic approach to contemporary problems. They do serve, however, to set the framework of Paul VI's suggestion for the establishment of a world fund fed by the economics of disarmament. They also show the real possibility of overcoming the underdevelopment that afflicts a large part of the human race at present, and of doing so quickly. What is quite clear is that as long as disarmament does not become a fact, international aid for development will languish at its present modest level, because it does not seem to be within the resources of any country to cope with a massive effort in development aid and preparations for war at the same time. A sufficient indication of this is the present balance of payments position of the United States, so heavily influenced by external military spending and its corresponding limitation of the amount that can be devoted to cooperation in development programs for the underdeveloped countries.

On the political level, this is one of those vicious circles that economists are accustomed to find on the level of economic development: expenditures on arms and defense paralyze a great mass of resources and reduce to a minimum the amount that can be devoted to development. This limitation prevents any massive effort to achieve economic expansion on a worldwide scale, and so maintains the conditions of underdevelopment that generate political and military tensions and lead to excessive expenditures on armaments.

The advances made since the end of World War II in the handling of international development aid and the creation of organs of international cooperation—for example, the World Bank, the Inter-American Development Bank (BID), the Inter-American Committee for the Alliance for Progress (CIAP), the Organization for Economic Cooperation and Development (OECD) and the various agencies of the United Nations—allow one to say that adequate means of channeling an increased volume of aid do exist. What is lacking now is the increased volume. It is the present modest scale of this volume that constitutes the problem, not the means of administering it.

2. *Conditions Governing Loans for Development*

Populorum progressio points to the need for "making an assessment of the contribution necessary, not only drawn up in terms of the generosity and the available wealth of the donor nations, but also conditioned by the real needs of the receiving countries and the use to which the financial assistance can be put. Developing countries will thus no longer risk being overwhelmed by debts whose repayment swallows up the greater part of their gains. Rates of interest and time for repayment of the loan could be so arranged as not to be too great a burden on either party, taking into account free gifts, interest-free or low-interest loans, and the time needed for liquidating the debts" (n. 54).

This suggestion is fully justified by the facts. In 1955 the total external debt of 97 developing countries was $10,000,000,000. By 1965 this had risen to $36,400,000,000. This is an annual increase of 14%. As a result, the developing countries have had to reserve increasing proportions of their export earnings to finance the repayments due on their external debts. In 1965 this proportion was 9%. This average disguises the situation of many developing countries which were forced to default on their loan repayments due to their internal economic situation, brought about by the excessive growth of their external debt.[10]

In Latin America the situation is as bad as that in the rest of the developing world, if not worse. In 1955 the total external debt of all the Latin American countries amounted to $4,300,000,000. By 1965 this had risen to $11,600,000,000. Moreover, in 1955 only 5% of export earnings were needed for repayments, but by 1965 this figure had risen to 15%.

This situation has its roots in the structure of the export trade

[10] World Bank, *op. cit.*

of developing countries and those on the periphery of the great industrial centers. The encyclical notes: "Highly industrialized nations export for the most part manufactured goods, while countries with less developed economies have only food, fibers and other raw materials to sell" (n. 57). It is a well-known fact that world exports of foodstuffs and raw materials grow much more slowly than those of manufactured goods. Between 1930 and 1960 the former (excluding oil) grew by 15% and the latter by 105%.

There are various reasons for this tendency. The first and most important is that the pattern of demand is modified with improving standards of living and growth of economic power. As this happens, for example, the demand for wheat is relatively lowered at the expense of an increasing demand for motor cars, chemical products, machinery and other equipment. The inevitable consequence is that the world demand for industrial products must grow faster than the demand for foodstuffs and raw materials. Technical progress has also decreased the demand for certain raw materials by finding synthetic substitutes for them and by increased productivity in putting them to use.

These tendencies, which are inherent in the process of development itself, have been backed up by the protectionist policies pursued by the industrial countries to boost their own production of cereals, livestock or other foods and raw materials. In the United States, for example, imports of the more important primary products (coffee, non-ferrous metals, textile fibers, etc.) increased between 1930 and 1960 by 17%, while actual consumption of the same categories increased by 35%. Home production, in other words, has been satisfying an increasingly large share of total demand.[11]

Therefore, peripheral countries concentrating on production of raw materials are bound to show a slower export growth rate. Their imports, on the other hand, grow rapidly because such imports are composed of industrial goods essential to their development and to the raising of their standard of living. Hence

[11] United Nations, *World Economic Report* (New York, 1959).

their exports and imports have a permanent tendency to greater and greater imbalance, and these countries incur an ever-mounting burden of debt inasmuch as their export earnings are insufficient to meet the bills for essential imports. Furthermore, the incidence of external debt on their balance of payments has tended to mount as the terms of international finance impose higher interest rates and shorter repayment periods. This tendency is seen in the declining proportion of loans made under non-commercial conditions and the increasing proportion of short- or medium-term loans used to promote the exports of the industrial countries which make the loans. It is interesting to note that in South America's case, 47% of the external debt is repayable in five years or less.

I will return to these questions in my remarks on the encyclical's proposals in the realm of commercial politics.

3. *Economic Cooperation between Neighboring Countries*

The encyclical expresses the hope that "the countries whose development is less advanced will be able to take advantage of their proximity in order to organize among themselves, on a broadened territorial basis, areas for concerted development, to draw up programs in common, to coordinate investments, to distribute the means of production and to organize trade" (n. 64). This proposal ties in with the conclusion reached by modern analysis of the problems of development that the formulation of wider market groups by several developing countries is a positive contribution to a more rational use of available resources and an acceleration of growth rate. Coordination of policy vis-à-vis the rest of the world would also strengthen their bargaining position. Economic integration is a particularly important instrument in the promotion of industrial development, especially of basic industries which have to operate on a large scale to be efficient.

Of the developing areas, Latin America is the one where the process of economic integration, while still on a modest scale, is so far most apparent. It is interesting to note that the encyclical's proposals concern not only the commercial aspects of integration ("to organize trade"), but also other important aspects such as the coordination of investments. All these points are being closely examined in Latin America, particularly in the context of the relationship between the nationalistic aspirations of each country and the integrated development of the whole region.[12] It is vital that these points should be clearly understood if the way is to be opened for an increased development rate in each country within the context of the Latin American economy as a whole. The encyclical's proposals are a help here in clearing the way and taking decisions in favor of development through integration.

4. *Commercial Policies in International Trade*

According to *Populorum progressio,* "in trade between developed and underdeveloped economies, conditions are too disparate and the degrees of genuine freedom available are too unequal". To correct this, it suggests a framework of international agreements sufficiently wide in scope: "They would establish general norms for regulating certain prices, for guaranteeing certain types of production and for supporting certain new industries" (n. 61).

The encyclical then proceeds to give examples and suggests that agreements concerning basic products should either be broadened or put into practice and that the industrial countries should liberalize their commercial policies with respect to their imports of foodstuffs and raw materials and give preference to manufactured goods exported by the developing countries.

"The poor nations remain ever poor while the rich ones become still richer." This can be seen to result from the fact that, in the words of the encyclical, "highly industrialized nations export for the most part manufactured goods, while countries with less developed economies have only food, fibers and other raw materials to sell" (n. 57). It should be asked if the damage suffered by the developing countries through this particular bias of their

[12] For a further treatment of some aspects of the question, see Ferrer, "Integracion latinoamericana y desarollo nacional," in *Comercio Exterior* (Banco Nacional de Comercio Exterior: Mexico, Mar. 1967).

economies is due solely to the restrictive commercial policies of the industrial nations, or whether the causes lie deeper. These policies obviously aggravate the problem, but the basic reason why some "become still richer" while others "remain ever poor" is the fact that the underdeveloped countries specialize in the production of foodstuffs and raw materials. I have already pointed out that technical progress and changing patterns of demand lead to a much slower growth rate in the consumption of foodstuffs and raw materials than in industrial goods. Those who specialize in the former and postpone the latter will always stay poor, while those whose industrial production occupies the central place that it should in their economies will benefit from an ever increasing growth rate and standard of living. It is possible to find exceptions to this general rule, but such exceptions do not affect its general validity for all developing countries.

It is not sufficient for the poorer nations to acquire a certain stage of development in the simpler branches of manufacturing. The dynamic of modern industrial development is based predominantly on the so-called heavy industries (engineering, heavy chemicals, paper, cellulose, etc.). United Nations estimates show that between 1948 and 1961 the world increase in heavy industry was 225% while that of light industry (food and drink, textiles, leather goods, etc.) was 168%.[13] The structure of world trade in manufactured goods shows similar tendencies. Long-term figures for the period 1899–1959 indicate that exports stemming from the main divisions of heavy industry (metallurgy, engineering, chemistry) accounted for 39% of the world's exports of manufactured goods in 1899, 50% in 1929 and 71% in 1959.[14]

Thus it will be seen that the introduction of heavy industry is an indispensable condition of participation in the more dynamic categories of world trade, with their corresponding high growth rate. Moreover, as technical and scientific progress is strongly

[13] United Nations, *The Growth of World Industry 1948–61* (New York, 1965).
[14] A. Maizels, *Industrial Growth and World Trade* (London, C.U.P., 1963).

linked to the industrial base of a country and the relative position occupied in its industry by those industries heaviest in capital and technological requirements, it follows that the expansion of heavy industry conditions a country's capacity to generate and absorb modern advances in knowledge.

There is little doubt that a more liberal policy on the part of the industrial nations with respect to their imports of foodstuffs and raw materials from the developing countries would make a significant contribution to their development. But practice points up the difficulties of putting this into effect. The result of the negotiations recently concluded by GATT in Geneva shows that, out of total tariff reductions that benefit world exports to the tune of $44,000,000,000, only $1,000,000,000 affect the peripheral countries. As has already been said, world trade is becoming more and more of a rich man's club affair, which is the same as saying that it is becoming increasingly confined to the highly industrialized nations.

Even if the industrialized nations do liberalize their policies, this will still not correct the deep-seated tendencies toward imbalance in modern economic development which lead to a relative decline in the status of primary produce. As a result, the unequal growth rates of rich and poor countries can only be evened out by a fundamental transformation of the pattern of production in the poor countries, with a basic shift toward expansion of industrial activity in general, and heavy industry in particular.

It is important to understand what is involved here. We are not denying the basic importance to the developing countries of increasing their output of foodstuffs and raw materials, as much to satisfy their own internal demand as for export. On the contrary, it is impossible to envisage a vigorous growth of industrial output and the economy in general without a substantial improvement in their level of alimentation and supply of livestock, minerals, etc. This inevitably entails a rapid increase in primary production alongside industry. What is involved is a recognition of the historically proved fact that overcoming the economic backwardness of two-thirds of the human race is incompatible with the maintenance of the traditional international division between industrial countries and those engaged in primary produce. Only through a rapid transformation of the pattern of production and economic expansion of the peripheral countries will it be possible to rearrange world trade and finances in such a way as to give these countries an equal share in a world which is growing continually more interdependent through the ever increasing growth of science and technology.

The encyclical's proposals with regard to commercial policy should, in my view, be taken in the wider context of its whole program for the overcoming of underdevelopment. This program is based on the fundamental need for all countries to make a radical effort to transform their economy in depth and modernize their economic and social structures, and the need for the developing countries to cooperate in this undertaking through the intensification of financial and technological aid to them. The formation of a great "World Fund", financed with the savings brought about through disarmament, and the provision of loans and grants appropriate in their scale and conditions to the present state of the "poor" countries are the central pivots round which a program of international cooperation for development must revolve.

III

THE PRINCIPLES GOVERNING A PROGRAM
OF INTERNATIONAL COOPERATION

Populorum progressio lays down two main principles necessary for the effective execution of an international plan for development: the need for individual effort and respect for each country's right to self-determination.

1. *Individual Effort*

"Guarantees could be given to those who provide the capital that it will be put to use according to an agreed plan and with a

reasonable measure of efficiency, since there is no wish to encourage parasites or the indolent" (n. 54). The same point is
made elsewhere by quoting the words of St. Paul: "If anyone will
not work, let him not eat" (2 Thess. 3, 10). But the encyclical
does recognize that conditions of human degradation can sometimes, as a result of underdevelopment, be such that individual
effort alone has no chance of tackling the problem. There are
regions "where the cares of day-to-day survival fill the entire existence of families incapable of planning the kind of work that
would open the way to a less desperate future. These, however,
are the men and women who must be helped and persuaded to
work for their own betterment and to endeavor to acquire gradually the means to that end" (n. 55).

Thus the encyclical clearly posits the need for individual effort
without falling into the simplistic trap of thinking that backwardness is a result of indolence. It makes clear at several points that
by individual effort it means particularly a change of attitude on
the part of those groups who, by their political influence and links
with establishments that have a vested interest in underdevelopment, paralyze all efforts at change and renewal. Where these
groups are in power, resources in the shape of outside help cannot
be used efficiently, and thus any program of international cooperation is seriously damaged.

2. The Right to Self-Determination

"The receiving countries could demand that there be no interference in their political life or subversion of their social structures. As sovereign States they have the right to conduct their
own affairs, to decide on their own policies and to move freely
toward the kind of society they choose. What must be brought
about, therefore, is a system of cooperation freely undertaken, an
effective and mutual sharing, carried out with equal dignity on
both sides, for the construction of a more human world" (n. 54).
"World solidarity, ever more effective, should allow all peoples
to become the artisans of their destiny; may . . . international
relations be marked with the stamp of mutual respect and friend-

ship, of interdependence in collaboration, and the betterment of all be seen as the responsibility of each individual" (n. 65).

In these passages the encyclical states that outside help should not compromise the right of any country receiving such aid to choose its own form of institutions ("to move freely toward the kind of society they choose"), to determine the strategy of its own development and to put it into effect without interference. Both aspects of the principle of self-determination are very important for the internal stability of each country and for international peace. If the industrialized countries which provide aid tie it to conditions governing the institutional and political organization of the recipients, they will not only create tensions and resistance there, but also arouse hostile reactions in other great powers which hold different ideological and political principles. If this happens, international aid, far from strengthening the internal security of the developing countries and peace, will lead to new sources of instability and conflicts of every kind. The same thing will happen when the countries or organizations providing aid try to dictate priorities in how the resources made available through aid are to be spent. These priorities must arise from the aspirations of each country in the economic and social orders and the sort of place it wants to occupy on the international scene. Whether or not the road chosen is in fact the one best suited to achieve the full economic development of each country will be discovered as the program is put into effect. The principle of individual effort must be respected, but of course each country has the duty to make the most efficient use possible of the resources allotted to it.

In order to avoid the risk of aid from one particular country to a single beneficiary being used to compromise the latter's self-determination, the encyclical proposes that development aid should be the product of collaboration among the industrial nations: "If they [the resources made available] were to be fitted into the framework of worldwide collaboration, they would be beyond all suspicion, and as a result there would be less distrust on the part of the receiving nations. These would have less cause for fearing that, under the cloak of financial aid or technical assistance, there lurk certain manifestations of what has come to be called neo-colonialism, in the form of political pressures and economic suzerainty aimed at maintaining or acquiring complete dominance" (n. 52). It only remains to add that the receiving nations should participate on an equal footing with the grantor nations in the administration of this program of worldwide collaboration. This is obviously an important condition if the objective proposed in the encyclical is to be achieved.

Philipp Herder-Dorneich/*Cologne, W. Germany*

How Can the Church Provide Guidelines in Social Ethics?

There is general agreement that the Church has an important role to play in the fashioning of economic and social processes. She *should* furnish socio-ethical guidelines upon which further decisions could be based. Both her members and many outsiders expect this of her. Therefore, this point will not be debated here.

It is also my assumption that the Church basically *can* provide such social and ethical guidelines, so I shall not linger over that point. But there is another question which has not yet been answered and which, indeed, has not really been posed: *How* is she to do this? This question is of a more practical nature; perhaps that is why many regard it as of lesser importance. But if the Church ignores such practical questions, she may be totally ineffective in trying to shape and develop society.

I

DECISION-MAKING AS A DUTY

Anyone who takes an active part in shaping our societal life—the employer, the union leader, the politician, the social scientist—is faced with decisions. Decision-making is the peculiar task of economic and social leaders. It is upon their decision-making ability that their prestige rests. This duty of making decisions, which cannot be sluffed off onto the shoulders of others, is a heavy burden, and requires that they must have guidelines upon which their decisions can be based.

Guidelines do not eliminate the need for making decisions, nor do they take away all risk, but they do make the decision-making process easier. What must be made clear at the outset is the fact that the person or party who lays down guidelines cannot replace the decision-maker in business and politics. Time and again this point has been brought out by management consultants, who have created a new and distinctive kind of service in recent years. They often find that their clients, whoever they may be, think that the consultants can eliminate the danger and risk of decision-making. This is not so; the only way to escape decision-making is to resign from a job that calls for decision-making.

Here we are concerned with decisions on questions of social ethics. In one sense, this does not really restrict the question too much; since business, economics and politics have to do with man, all decisions in these areas are socio-ethical decisions. But here we are not concerned with day-to-day business problems; we are concerned with a particular aspect of decision-making. Let me illustrate what I mean with a few examples.

Sample Cases

We talk about competition and its anonymous hand inexorably separating the wheat from the chaff. Competition is an economic phenomenon. What form competition takes, however, is up to the decision of individual business leaders. They can compete fairly with each other in terms of efficiency, or they can try to cut each other's throats. What seems to be a purely economic matter takes on socio-ethical overtones when we ask: What methods are to be employed in the process of competition? We are suddenly at the *borderline* of ethics, and this area can be decisive in trying to delimit a full business ethics.

Let me give another example. An employer may suddenly feel obliged to let some employees go. On the surface, it is purely a matter of economics. Sales are shrinking, so production must be cut down and less employees will be needed. But is that all that is involved?

When we take a closer look, we see that there is more to it. The concrete decision does have a socio-ethical aspect. Which employees are to be laid off—men or women, citizens or foreign workers? Should they all be laid off at once so that it can be called a mass layoff and entitle the employees to public unemployment benefits? Or should it be done in stages, which may make it difficult for them to collect unemployment benefits from public sources?

How are we to approach such questions? Where can we find guidelines that will make it easier for us to reach decisions on such matters? Until recently it was said that an answer lay close at hand. We were told that the principles of Catholic social doctrine provided us with the necessary guidelines upon which to act.

II

CATHOLIC SOCIAL DOCTRINE

Stage 1: The Classical Period

As we began to construct a free society in Germany after World War II, Catholic social doctrine was presented to us as a catalogue of *hard and fast* norms, set down *a priori*. It was a solid, cast-iron framework, with a peg for any individual problem that might come up, and it was rooted in the nature of things, which never changed.

When we look back on that classical period today, we are struck by the wealth of pronouncements, based on natural law, which went into detail on every issue. Natural law included not only first principles, but also all corollaries which were deduced from these principles.

What remains of all this now? The corollaries and deductions, with all their subtleties, have been relegated to the archives of history. What continues to endure is the natural law, man's obligation to take responsibility for others *as he works out his life.* Man is not programmed in advance by nature. He is placed in history, and he must work out a concrete pattern of life by coming to grips with the throes of historical existence.

Human nature is not that of a ready-made being. It is not handed to man; it is put into his hands. Man is a "being that can be", not a "being that is there" from the start. He is entrusted with the task of fashioning himself; this is the tie which binds him to his creator. This moral imperative cannot be proved; it can only be pointed out phenomenologically. It involves *three* elements: selfhood, relations with others and creaturehood. The latter element is brought in if one does not want to restrict his considerations to the purely natural level. By virtue of this imperative, man is entrusted to his own hands; he is to interpret his own self and the world of changing relationships in which he is involved.

Using the eyes of faith, and ever attentive to the testimony of Scripture, the Church must now spell out and concretize the law of love in the various strata of man's cultural life. It is here that the Church must join in the dialogue concerning temporal structures and designs. It is not for her to fashion any definitive social or economic system. Her task is to test any and every temporal structure in terms of the data of theological anthropology. Her ethical mission is precisely this: to take seriously the arrangement which God has ordained for man in the Christ-event.

This unavoidable mission of the Church is not under question here. Our concern is of a more practical nature: How is she to formulate and deliver social and ethical guidelines that meet the demands of a concrete social and economic order?

Stage 2: Vatican Council II

The classical period of Catholic doctrine abruptly ended with the death of Pius XII. The braintrust upon which he had depended, and in which German Jesuits had played an important role, was relegated to the background. New specialists took their place and helped to formulate *Mater et Magistra.*

Catholic doctrine now ceased to be the all-encompassing thing it had once been. It began to break down into individual pronouncements on concrete situations. The new encyclical retained the general, all-embracing tone of earlier social encyclicals, but it was clearly addressed not so much to all the faithful as to particular groups—e.g., the landed aristocracy in Italy.

The transition from comprehensive pronouncements to special directives and admonitions was only logical. The world had become a complex place with many and varied levels. No problem existed everywhere in quite the same cast. The new focus on specific concrete situations, of course, called for much specialized knowledge. The social philosopher would now need the social scientist and the man experienced in practical social matters; otherwise, the conclusions would be of little value.

Vatican Council II took cognizance of this need. Besides using theological specialists, it also invited lay specialists to attend. When we look back on the conciliar period today, we can easily see how it departed from the procedure of the classical period. *Concern for concrete realities* began to displace abstract speculation on the natural law.

Suppose we pursue this line of development to its ultimate conclusions. Is it possible that natural law simply means "in accordance with objective realities"? If so, then the social architect, who is trying to fashion a social order, would resemble the building architect. The latter, using new materials, develops new building designs; the former, using the new pattern of social relations that exists, tries to fashion a social order. All he has to do is to explore the full connections and have full knowledge of the realities at hand to do a good job. In other words, only the *uninitiate* believe that real decision-making is involved. In fact, as one explores the facts more closely, the proper course becomes readily apparent.

Undoubtedly, much remains to be done in developing this grasp of the objective situation. The social sciences are far behind the natural sciences in this respect; they have much catching up to do. But it will become evident time and again that the logic of the situation will suggest the proper answer.

However, the process of objective analysis will not totally eliminate the need for decision-making. Let me cite two reasons for this:

1. When we deal with the social order, we are always dealing in the future, and the future is unknown. In many instances we must act without full knowledge of the real situation because it would cost too much to acquire this knowledge. It is theoretically possible, for example, to do exhaustive market research on a new product. But, speaking practically, this is so costly and time-consuming that only a few products merit this much attention. In most instances, we must resort to trial-and-error techniques. We put the product on the market and watch what happens.

2. Social realities are not only unknown; they are also undetermined. Individuals and social groups are historical realities. They change over the course of time, and these changes basically are not subject to human reckoning.

Now if we take these two limitations into account, we can make the following assertions about social analysis. In many instances we can say what is *not* possible; only rarely can we positively determine what must inevitably happen. In other words, expert analysis can make negative determinations with relative ease; with some difficulty it can also describe alternative possibilities that are equally feasible; only rarely, in highly controlled situations, can it arrive at clear determinations. Expert knowledge delimits the field of decision-making, but it rarely eliminates the need for decision itself.

Stage 3: The Post-Conciliar Period

Now we come to the present post-conciliar period. What problems have come to the fore and what are their consequences?

The best way to approach this question is to consider the recent encyclical *Populorum progressio*. Here again we are dealing with a social encyclical. Here again the encyclical is talking about a worldwide social problem, not about a purely national one. Its concern is the progress of underdeveloped nations. Two things are striking: its concern for the temporal aspects of the world and its use of modern ideas and forms of expression. Instead of the old curial style, we find short, incisive sentences, and the central topic—economic and social development—is given sharp focus from the very beginning. Noteworthy also is the fact that *Populorum progressio* was originally composed in French, and that its outlook and style of thought has an almost wholly French approach. What are we to deduce from this?

The radically different outlook of *Populorum progressio* is a very interesting development, and quite understandable. The shift from abstract speculation to expert analysis, which was given impetus by Vatican Council II, created a need for specialists and experts on specific topics. These experts, having ready access to the curial apparatus, bring their theories with them and inject them into the encyclical being written. Such theories and conceptions are founded on sound knowledge of the subject, but, as we saw above, they are not completely objective. Personal views and conclusions are also intertwined.

Today there is much *intellectual lobbying*. Ideas and viewpoints are competing for men's minds. If we are to understand Catholic social doctrine today, we must understand how such doctrine is now being formulated.

Today opinions are *molded*. They develop out of the clash of contrasting and opposing ideologies. They are propounded in the marketplace of ideas and put across by the lobbying of powerful interests. The process of molding and controlling public opinion, which was once a dark secret, is now becoming clear and comprehensible. It is a good thing, because the process itself is necessary and inevitable. To deprecate it would be to misconstrue the needs of the present day.

In a changing world we have a constant need for new ideas, new opinions and new experiences. These things do not just happen; they are the fruit of hard work. They are fashioned by a host of thinkers, practical men and experts. The greater the number of people involved in this process, the better the chance for satisfactory results.

But how is this process operating in the area of Catholic social doctrine? What is the *modus operandi?* In the case of *Populorum progressio,* we do not know. We do not know who the author was, or what advisers were involved. We do not know if the opinions of dissenting experts were given consideration. We do not know who chose the authors and advisers, or how they were chosen.

Herein lies the critical problem for the present stage in the development of Catholic social doctrine. If sound experts must be called in to develop it further, who is to select them? Furthermore, who decides which opinion shall be heard?

III

THE NEED FOR STRUCTURED DIALOGUE

Pluralism presupposes a properly ordered framework of competition. When we ask the social sciences what experiences are pertinent here, economics provides us with the first key. Economists point to the significance of games theory in societal life. They stress that pluralism (of opinions and values) must be dependent on game rules and the verification they provide. A person or a group can claim the right of leadership and demand a decisive role only by proving the exercise of the requisite leadership in the framework of a structured competitive process.

Competition among Ideas in Catholicism

Now let us relate this to the realm of the Church. Is the Church structured in such a way that she can vindicate her claim to make pronouncements on social questions?

In the classical period, as we saw, a handful of theologians were authorized by institutional officials to elaborate Catholic social doctrine through encyclicals. Later on, Vatican Council II made use of experts and published constitutions on social issues.

This represented an important step forward because it broadened the base of underlying opinions and hence the formulative process, even though no great doctrinal development on social questions ensued.

When we consider the present approach being used today, we can only regard it as a step backward. A small group of theologians were responsible for the social theories of *Populorum progressio,* and similar small groups in Germany are formulating ideas which subsequently are published under Church auspices. This is a step backward because the pluralistic base has been shrunk, and because no real legitimate basis for these socio-economic, non-theological ideas is offered.

How can we begin to move forward again? Natural law can no longer be regarded as universally binding when it is a question of specific, concrete issues. Catholic social doctrine must find a *new way to prove its validity.* As of now, most pronouncements have degenerated to the level of personal opinions, and such opinions of themselves cannot have binding force. They acquire this force only if we know what group stands behind them. We must broaden the pluralistic base involved in the formulation of such opinions.

Catholic social doctrine is now irrevocably enmeshed in the pluralism of present-day opinion-molding. It is involved in a process of debate and dialogue, *and this dialogue, this debate, must be conducted in a structured way.* A social pronouncement can claim authoritativeness only if it results from the competitive process proper to opinion-shaping today. Socio-political opinions which pose as authoritative pronouncements soon lose any vestige of authority.

Social Doctrine as Socio-Political Dialogue

How, then, can the Church provide socio-ethical guidelines? How can she help us to make decisions? Basically, it seems she can do this in one of two ways:

1. The Church can formulate pronouncements and directives which spell out what must be done in a given situation. In other

words, she can set down *positive norms*. In our pluralistic and rapidly changing world, however, it seems that she would rarely deal with a situation properly by using this approach.

2. The Church can provide a *forum* in which those who hold many and varied opinions can engage in dialogue with each other. She would not point out what is to be done. Instead, she would enable all to discuss the problems together and thus work out a decision. This is what she would contribute to the decision-making process. Vatican Council II has set dialogue in motion within the Church, but this dialogue has not yet been given a formal structure within her institutions. The present is an opportune time to fashion such structures.

It seems to me that we should pursue this second approach with some of the zeal that was once applied to the first approach. The goal of Catholic social teaching should be the formation of a structured dialogue with Catholic society—e.g., between the hierarchy and the laity.

Basic Rules for the Dialogic Process

The structuring of socio-political dialogue in the Church cannot be accomplished on the drawing-board. It must take its impetus from historical situations and possibilities. The lessons which the social sciences have to teach—about competition, games theory, etc.—must be given due consideration. Economics and political science have many important contributions to make in this area.

It would be a mistake, I think, to entrust to theologians primarily the task of structuring this dialogue. Nor is it sufficient to give theologians special training in the social sciences. *It is not just a question of using expert, scholarly doctrine; it is also a question of exploring in depth the experiences of the economist and the social scientist.*

In terms of historical realities, the structuring of this dialogue should not be swayed too greatly by *political forces*. Catholic social teaching, as the structuring of a dialogue, should focus on historical forces that operate beyond the borders of provincialism and nationalism. There is great danger that political forces will regard this dialogue as a "Catholic parliament" and ensconce themselves within it. Nothing much will be gained if political parties and vested interests insinuate their representatives into such forums to lobby for their special viewpoints. *The fields covered in this Catholic dialogue should not coincide with political lines of demarcation.*

While all historical forces should be mobilized in this process, our gaze must not be directed backward. Dialogue is a new secular reality in the Church. It should catch the gust of a fresh wind and sail forward into the future.

It is important, I think, to pay heed to newly developing institutions and not to remain too sentimentally attached to the revered institutions of the past. The diocese is a time-honored institution; its regional structure is centuries old. But its venerable age does not ensure its adaptability to dialogue.

Vatican Council II gave new life and impetus to the episcopal conferences and their activities. New tasks and new sources of strength are taking shape. These new institutions are not so strongly impregnated with the authoritative forms of the past. It is probably easier to give these new institutions a dialogic form than to remold the old institutions.

If the episcopal conferences are to be successful, I think it is important that a lay council be added to them, and we should not start at the parochial or diocesan level in fashioning such councils.

We want to attract the *most qualified* lay people to the lay advisory boards, and to attract top people, we must offer them challenging and important assignments. Top talent wants to sink its teeth into challenging problems. Thus we must necessarily compete with the challenges offered by secular professions. *The possibilities and opportunities for activity in the Catholic realm should match those in the secular realm.*

The same holds true for monetary compensation. The people involved will have to expend time and effort, and they should receive appropriate monetary compensation. Those who are active in these social questions should be able to live off their labors, as any professional man does. We must rid ourselves of the delusion that the problems of the future can be solved by "honorary" chairmen who are not paid for their work.

Involvement in Catholic lay councils must be a professional line of work. This means that they must be organized on higher levels than the diocesan or the provincial councils because the latter do not have adequate financial resources. Presumably, at the level of episcopal conferences, there would be projects of great magnitude and continuing importance; hence social institutions and organizations would take it upon themselves to send qualified people to these Catholic organisms.

When the problems are of great moment and gravity, organizations and institutions would presumably want to select and send qualified representatives to the deliberations. In such instances, the problem of selection and remuneration would be settled by the companies themselves.

This raises the inevitable problem of a possible takeover by outside interests. Long experience has shown how often outside bodies have obtained a foothold in Catholic councils and then diverted their operations to suit vested interests. It is also evident that lay activity in such councils is dependent on such things as the available budget and the scope of activity permitted.

When we talk about qualified people here, we must not be tied down to the outlook and prejudices of an older social order. We should not think solely about men of wealth or "big names". What we need in these lay councils is not famous writers and theologians but competent specialists in specific fields who know their job. Their task in these councils will be to serve as spokesmen for a professional point of view.

We must divest ourselves of the delusions of the past. *We should not be afraid of conflict and debate in the dialogic process.* If we force these lay specialists to use Latin or to keep their deliberations secret, a fruitful dialogue will never get off the ground. If we are afraid to leave room for one-sided viewpoints, we shall not leave room for any viewpoints at all. In short, *we must not shun conflict and debate. We must leave room for conflict in our dialogues and give this conflict a dialogic structure.*

Lay representatives to such councils must validate their right to be present by some sort of *elective process.* Here the lessons of political science regarding elective procedures must be evaluated seriously. One basic lesson is this: a single election does not ensure authentic representation. Only a series of elections, mutually complementing one another and spread out over at least one generation, will prove to be functionally adequate.

Representative procedures must be developed with deliberateness and logical consistency. *The ecumenical council, which met for a short time and then disbanded again, does not provide us with the right model in this area.*

I have tried to spell out some of the practical considerations which must be taken into account if the Church is to provide socio-ethical guidelines. The tasks before us are urgent ones, and they call for our active involvement. We cannot treat them in a dilettante fashion. We must make full use of past experience, whether it be the experience of theologians or of technical experts.

Janko Musulin/*Vienna, Austria*

Races and Minorities:
A Matter of Conscience

When the inherent danger of war in the Cyprus conflict created unrest in the world at large, it pointed up not only the inexorable nature of the old minority conflict but also how such a conflict involves international politics. The relations between Athens and Ankara and the interests of the United States, England and the countries of the Atlantic alliance were all linked up with it. In spite of this the problems of races and minorities are generally looked upon as isolated issues. In doing so one not only overlooks the fact that these problems have become a decisive factor in world politics but also that there is here a constant mutual interdependence. This becomes soon evident when one thinks, for instance, of the crew of the aircraft carrier Roosevelt who declined to enter a South African port because the conditions implied racial discrimination. Such an incident clearly indicated that the racial problem of the States was connected with that of South Africa. But the lasting context, the permanence of this mutual effect, was barely recognized.

The Consequences of Tabooism

All this is not accidental. The destruction or decimation of minorities in Europe when it was occupied by the armies of the Third Reich led to a taboo treatment of the question in that one

93

could discuss the past, but not the future. Something frightful had taken place on this occasion; one should face it and understand it. Insofar as the future was concerned, it was enough to show a horror of the crime and a simple good will.

Not all the consequences were harmful. The racial troublemaker, whose essential features have been investigated by Adorno in his *The Authoritarian Personality* (New York, 1950), yields to the social taboo and his aggressive disposition falls into the background. One might think that this taboo of the color issue would only hold true in continental Europe, but this is not so. It also spread to England where this silence was only broken in 1958. At first, little mention was made about the problem of the opposition that in a brief space of time rose so sharply against the colored people who had increased to over a million. But in 1965 this taboo still lingered on. Thus an American visitor wrote in the magazine *Race* about his conversations with trade unionists in Greater London: "During my talks I noticed that people generally declined to speak about the color problem as such." However understandable the rise of this taboo and however useful some of its consequences, one cannot overlook the fact that it encouraged a certain illusory comfort, a certain lack of interest, with regard to what does not concern one immediately.

In a world where communication has been so extraordinarily intensified and where events that take place in the most varied parts of the world influence one another with such lightning speed, the notion of the "neighbor" who must be "loved like oneself" can no longer be interpreted in exactly the same way as at the beginning of the Industrial Revolution or the agricultural societies out of which the present age developed. The commandment must be interpreted in a broader sense; it embraces new duties and new tasks, not least among which are duties to inform oneself and to face new situations which did not exist before. The first soundings, however, show that most Christians, if they can no longer escape a confrontation of these issues, betray in their very vocabulary and terminology an uncertainty which makes them fall back on arguments which are wholly out of touch with the present situation, and take refuge in a peculiarly defensive attitude.

The Starting Point

This phenomenon is definitely connected with the fact that the new development of some races and the problem of minorities remained concealed for the reasons given above, and that when these issues penetrated into the awareness of the public and could no longer be avoided, they assumed correspondingly larger proportions. The sudden confrontation contained an element of fear which led to a wish to suppress them. Could it really be already so serious again? Where did we fail? Were all our good intentions futile, and is it merely a matter of fate, something that besets us constantly?

One of the most bitter ironies of world history is that, in a practically secluded and acute minority situation—which was in itself no worse in its division than that which prevailed in India at the time of the partition—national socialism resorted to bloody measures, while as a consequence of this movement, but also as the result of war, regrouping and unrest, real racial and minority problems arose all over the world and are still springing up. These problems sharpen the old issues and make constructive solutions more difficult.

In Western Europe and the region influenced by it, the main cause is the increased mobility of capital and labor which has provoked shifts in the population at home and has created minority problems. The best investigated example of this factor is that of the "guest-workers" in Germany, a group more than a million strong, and the theater of the great minority tragedy of 1939–45 is of course carefully watched. We know little about the movement of populations in Russia and the Eastern bloc. There was a time when one heard constantly of Chinese coolies, workers or settlers in what used to be German territory. The way in which people reacted to such news at that time may have been dominated by the wish that such appropriated territory would be difficult to populate in any case.

A true picture of the situation is shown in the vast movements of peoples, national units and minorities within Communist territory. These show various causes: punitive measures, vast industrial projects, the exploitation of new land, strategic planning and change of the infrastructures. With the increase of liberalization the issues which so far have been played down will come to the fore again with all their peculiarities, as one can see already in Yugoslavia. Among these issues, that of how various nationalities can live together is the most important. Insofar as the rest of the world is concerned—that is, the world outside Europe—two factors must be pointed out first of all: decolonization and, connected with this, the rise of a vast number of new States and aid for their development.

Decolonization has not by itself created new minority problems, but it has sharpened the existing ones acutely; everywhere in Africa today there are refugees who belong to all kinds of minorities and bear eloquent witness to a situation where the old antagonisms are no longer contained by the colonial power. However unattractive such a situation may be when closely observed, it nevertheless exercises an influence on other regions. It accelerates the tempo of the American conflict and whips up the impatience of the American Negro. As Martin Luther King put it very clearly: "For three hundred and forty years we have been waiting for our God-given and constitutionally guaranteed rights. With the swiftness of a jet plane nations have achieved their independence in Africa and Asia, while we are still crawling along with the speed of a stage-coach in order to establish the right to get a cup of tea in a refreshment bar!" It also has a retarding influence on the situation in South Africa and Rhodesia because it has strengthened the whites in their fear of development and makes them seek their salvation in blocking every way that may lead to evolutionary progress.

Development Aid

While decolonization brought a wholly new meaning to old minority conflicts, the assistance given by the great industrialized nations to the underdeveloped countries seems to create a new form of minority conflict. In most cases this development aid is bound to break up a traditional agricultural society. The old egalitarian "sharing" society, the "poverty-sharing community", must yield to a more dynamic society based on distribution of labor, differences of income and subsidy. A process which it took Europe many centuries to complete must here be achieved in one single movement. This demands first of all the creation of a kind of native middle class which must be prized out of the ancient structures of society. This new class must be made familiar with a wholly new living standard and a new set of values; this will create a conflict with the older, more conservative community, which is looking for other ways of changing by itself. In the Mau-Mau rebellion the main victims were the Kikuyus who were already more modern in outlook. The same situation held true in the Congo troubles; however, these were complicated by the revival of intertribal rivalries. Basically the war in Vietnam reveals the same phenomenon: when a village is seized by the Vietcong, the victims are again mainly that middle class, the difference being that the attackers are not simply representing the old order but are equipped with the modern methods of a fighting elite.

Those concerned have already been aware for a long time of the doubts inherent in their situation. It is part of the dilemma of development aid that many colored students in developed countries do not want to return. When one insists on their return, one is suspected of discrimination; when one accepts the fact that they stay, one also has to accept that the aid provided has failed to achieve its end.

The Accelerated Pace of History

The first data of the problem can therefore be summarized as follows. The new or the more acute old conflicts can be reduced to some quite specific recognizable causes. These causes naturally include remnants of old antagonisms but cannot be identified with them. Further, individual causes are native and not interdependent, but the phenomena themselves are interdependent and exercise a mutual influence. The question is whether, in spite of very different causes, there is not a common factor which can explain the increasingly dangerous situation.

One should also be informed about the differences between the phenomena. In looking for an answer, we are soon hampered by the fact that the intensification of the conflict runs parallel with the increasingly rapid changes in technology and methods of production. One suspects that too much is being asked of man's adaptability. One would have to show obviously whether and how this overtaxing, this constant compulsion to improvise, sharpens so tragically the conflicts besetting people living in a state of constant dissolution and transformation.

It seems to be a fact that whenever man's inner constitution can no longer assimilate the speed with which these processes take place, fear (*Angst*) is born—uncontrolled, unbridled fear which it is difficult to bring to the conscious surface, particularly where the changes are rational and constructive (raising the standard of living, for instance). Perhaps it is the high fear content in modern society which makes it prone to catastrophe. Fear turns into aggressiveness and combines with the usual inclination to reject. And so man turns against what is foreign, other, unknown, against men of another mode of speech, another pigmentation, another system of values.

The History of Racism

If one looks for the answer to the question as to which phenomena are new and characteristic of our age, one finds first of all that it is impossible to make a clear distinction between racial problems and minority problems. The prejudice lies already embedded in the use of the terms. All racial problems are of course also minority problems, but there are many minority problems that have nothing to do with race. Thus the so-called "racially persecuted" of the various compensation laws belong in fact to a persecuted minority. This certainly holds for the Jews; even the trials of Nuremberg were not based on racial characteristics but on the confessional antecedents, and scientists agree that, in the static, genetic sense of the word—the Third Reich spoke of a "pure inheritance"—the term cannot be applied to the Jews.

Nor is the racial issue by any means the centuries-old fact which it is often said to be. The British statesman and historian, Lord Brice, has rightly pointed out that there was practically no conscious racism in any country before the French Revolution. People did not look at each other in terms of ethnology. The basis of this theory was laid only in the 19th century. It was then that people began to mix ethnological statements with linguistic ones; Gobineau wrote his four volumes on the inequality of human races, Houston Stewart Chamberlain began to exercise his influence, and in America the Ku Klux Klan was formed.

In historical fairness one must add that the fathers of racism had no idea of the catastrophic events to which their teaching and their views contributed. The first half of the 20th century was marked by this process of superficial vulgarization and brutalization. The second half, on the other hand, seems to show another kind of reciprocity: over against the original racialism there appears a second kind; over against the myth of superiority there is now a myth of inferiority; "white supremacy" is confronted by "black power"; instead of the picture of an Arian race that came to the fore in Europe, there has arisen in America the notion of the black man as the bearer of real culture; the superior attitude of the white Raj is now faced in Asia by the arrogance of color. One day this secondary kind of racialism, the racialism from below, may well become the greater evil.

Attitude toward the Race and Minority Issues

The lack of a penetrating understanding of the new problems related to races and minorities can only increase the difficulty of finding the right attitude from the Christian point of view. The extreme situation is simple and easily grasped: when the house of a neighbor who belongs to a minority group is set on fire and his very life is threatened, there can be no hesitation, and whatever one does will be less determined by theoretical arguments than by physical possibility, preparedness for heroism, or the interests of other persons, perhaps one's own family. But such an extreme case is always the last link in a very long chain of actions and omissions. The further one wants to go back along this chain, away from the actual terrifying event—which is not of course a simple straight line—the more ambivalent are the alternatives, the more doubtful the decisions, and the more frequently will one come upon situations where one might apparently have the choice of one type of reaction or another while in fact one has already opted for regression.

When one is familiar with the problems of minorities and races, one finds that in relatively frequent cases one has to admit that Christians hold questionable views, or at least show a certain hesitation. And so one fears that they will not be able to stand up to all dangerous situations in the long run. The reasons in depth for this vary a great deal and it is not at all easy to lay them bare. First of all, one meets with remnants of the old tabooism which is linked up with the aversion to what is "unhappy" in literature, journalism, etc. If the term "minority problem" is perhaps too innocuous in that it still allows of a relatively high interest, the terms "racial problem" and "racial conflict" remind people of the gruesome and fearful lessons of the past which they had succeeded in putting behind them. Older people particularly like to say that they had nothing to do "with all those things" and cannot now concern themselves with them. And if such questions nevertheless crop up in the conversation, a new aspect of tabooism and "not wanting to be disturbed" shows itself: one leaves it to the so-called experts or quite simply to those that "were there" or "live there". They do not realize that they always refer to representatives of a specific class, as in the case of South Africa. People who "live there" in no way try to see the problem as a whole but argue from their specific level of interests.

It is precisely local views and observation that are badly in need of complementary insights and information on such questions. When one has traveled in the southern States of the U.S.A. or has spoken to local inhabitants, one is aware of the kind of enlightened, rather more liberal than racially inclined citizen who emphasizes that "in his city" or "his region" everybody lives in the greatest harmony and that tensions between white and black are unknown—until there are demonstrations and "those young troublemakers" (freedom fighters, etc.) come in. In most cases there is no need to doubt the correctness of such an observation; yet the data of the opinion polls clearly show, even in the southern States, that this controversial activity nevertheless operates in the direction of a change in general opinion, a shift toward greater normality.

It is typical of these phenomena that local experiences accentuate different points from regional experiences. The process of normalization often passes through a phase of provocative extremism which spends itself in some last convulsions and is then discredited. If we may still have to deal here with general "defense mechanisms", which one can see in agnostics as much as in believers, the doubt about one's own Christian past is certainly a specific phenomenon.

In his voluminous work *Gottes Erste Liebe* (*God's First Love*) Friedrich Heer was not the first to seize upon this theme; it had been discussed before him. The arguments of this kind of mentality are still constantly brought into the discussion, and his systematic summary of them seems to have clarified the atmosphere rather than poisoned it. But when one starts not with Church history but with the minority problems, there is of course another basic situation, if only because in that case there is a rich amount of matter available for comparison in the regions dominated by other religions. It is significant to reflect on the fact that one of the greatest tragedies of the minority problem in our age, the conflict between Hindus and Moslems, involved two religious communities whose concepts are little inclined toward such catastrophes of fanaticism. Hinduism can be understood as a situation of tolerant and religious suspense. Joseph Mason said that "it rather refuses to define itself; there is something ultimate, some reality, in the general Hindu view, but to want to pin down this common possession of the truth to a 'this' or 'that' contradicts the very heart of Hinduism, because for the Hindu truth remains essentially and constantly in movement, according to the law of 'Karma' which is without end".

But before the outbreak of the catastrophic events Mohammed-anism also moved constantly in the direction of that tolerance which was formulated in the second *surah* of the Koran: "There must be no coercion in religion. Truth distinguishes itself from error." It is not difficult to draw the lesson from the communal tragedy of the Indian subcontinent, since the remaining evidence points in the same direction: the conflict is rooted in the religious element; it takes over certain outward elements, signs, gestures, formularies and legends from the prevalent confession, but the link between the raw primary effect and its religious alienation remains always recognizable as a prop; there is no possible fusion.

From these considerations about the connection between "religion" and "minority problems"—the overlap just mentioned of course does not weaken the argument—to the explanation of the basic causes is but one step. If it is not the religious element or the racial element (only racists can hold this view), what then is it?

This question is of more than theoretical importance: the right attitude of every individual is linked with the interpretation of the primary causes. But here we have to deal with a series of very ordinary, and not demonic, features which we all share individually, and which we cannot shake off without more ado. There is the unpleasant feeling we have toward the un-familiar (linked with the image of joy at what is familiar and the glow it bestows on notions like "home", "homeland", etc.), the bad temper roused by sounds that are meaningless to us, the suspicion of other notions about values, the fear of economic competition (the image of worry about income, about the fam-ily, etc.). Here the rational and the irrational are mixed in a way which can only be explained by a better knowledge of previous history. It might be summarized by saying that union with a larger group probably implies the exclusion of individuals belonging to other groups; when then further groups are joining up, the defense mechanism may weaken but not in such a way that all its functions vanish without exception. And so, in all racial and minority conflicts, one can feel the mechanisms of an earlier stage in development, mechanisms which are compatible with wholly rational observations, such as when a new arrival on the business scene shows a special talent which makes the older established employees feel ill at ease or even threatened. It is important to see such a typical connection, since today people occasionally are inclined to class as prejudice any observation with a negative point of view.

Thus, in an inquiry about the "guest workers" (foreign labor) in Germany, the question was asked whether the new arrivals were not "terribly loud"; one got the impression that an affirmative reply pointed to prejudice. But the only indication of prejudice here seems to be the popular adverb "terribly". It is possible that these workers are indeed more vocal and joyful and less preoccupied than the participants in the inquiry.

The Perfection of Tolerance

If one is aware of the previous history, if one remembers that the attitudes so easily mobilized against minorities are widespread, common, in no way particularly demonic, and able to be found in any combination or degree in almost all people, and if one understands further that only their vast collective multiplication can release aggression on the customary lines of old atrocities, one will discover, and avoid, another source of mistakes. If indifference, the tendency not to get involved, or to leave the responsibility to others and to rely, without any personal effort, on questionable experts or politicians, is the only evil, there is at the other end of the scale a puritanical idealism, a kind of pride, an impatience at the service of patience which can no longer be reconciled with humility. Perhaps one should see himself as a potential aggressor, a concealed disturber of the communal peace, before he can judge, understand and go to work on the problem.

Without this kind of self-accusation it is impossible to maintain a clear attitude which is strong enough to hold its own in the midst of life. Here the "love your neighbor like yourself" assumes a new dimension. In fact the ideology of tolerance seems somewhat unrealistic and fictitious and may even lose what has so far been achieved because of primitive and repetitive patterns of action. The plain "yes" of the "purist" to the famous question "Would you like your daughter to have a Negro husband?" is not very convincing. One does not yield to prejudice when one takes one's own existence into account, or when one takes note of a world where prejudice has spread and where the disapproval of the community with which one is ultimately concerned may not exclude but certainly reduce the chances of the success of such a marriage. For then the pretended satisfaction could only mean that it is based on fitting the fate of an individual—a closely related individual in this case—into a particular ideology that suits one's purposes, and this is not even human. If one would reply to that malicious question more intelligently, he would have to examine the question of opposition or support, to what extent he is prepared to identify himself with the choice once it is made, and how much love and understanding he thinks himself ultimately to be capable of.

It is still worse when not only the prejudice is ignored but no account is taken of concrete circumstances which are bound to stir up prejudice violently after a time. The way in which the color question developed in England is a good example of this situation and its causes. As long as Britain ruled a formidable colored empire, the average Englishman could pass a whole day without seeing a colored man. But this changed when the Empire became a Commonwealth, a situation soon recognized to be a passing phase which had to lead to a final solution.

The British Nationality Act of 1948 put the inhabitants of the Commonwealth on a par with the English, yet there was no methodical assessment of the many people who came into the country. In 1951 the number of colored people had grown to seventy thousand; from 1955 on they were counted, and since

1962 certain controls have been introduced. In 1965 1.5% of the population was colored, and before the end of the century the proportion will be similar to that in the United States. But during the whole of the first phase little was done about examining the problems implied in immigration, schools, housing and labor. Even the trade union leaders who must have known what happened on the factory floor took refuge in "purist" platitudes.

Today, however, a generation of colored Britishers is leaving school, and the Parliamentary Secretary for Home Affairs who is in charge of integration had to point out bluntly: "Unless we manage to create the infrastructure and solve our problems, we shall have to face the danger of white racial hatred and black militancy."

This, then, is the consequence of years of silence during which anyone who objected, wanted to introduce a quota system and to bring the movement under control was *a priori* suspected of racism. The Labor Party, which had itself condemned the Commonwealth Immigrants Act as discrimination, applies this act itself as a matter of course because it has understood the effects of a further increase of colored people on domestic peace at a time of increasing unemployment. If one thinks of the close links between England and Europe, and remembers that India and Pakistan settled their differences not in Oxford or Brighton, but in Tashkent, one wonders whether the educated immigrant from Sweden, Switzerland, Spain or Austria should not consider himself as discriminated against when he has to wait for years for his naturalization while an illiterate from the Punjab, a fisherman from Ceylon or a peasant from Madras, even today, after a few months, has both the active and passive vote and the same rights as any other citizen, even if he does not wish to take advantage of them.

When one understands that the Christian attitude toward races and minorities derives from the command of love of neighbor in a way which is differentiated, realistic and adjusted to the given circumstances, and that it cannot be the sense of the command to impose dogmatically the extreme implications of it, other questions arise. Can we rest satisfied with the prevention of catastrophes? Is it enough to alleviate the cruel circumstances which prevail in many parts of South Africa? Is it enough to study the tensions which occur every summer with frightening regularity in the United States, to do away with the social evils which create them, and to neglect situations that resemble a civil war? Is all this not too little, however important *per se?*

It is a curious fact that the idea which a minority has about its position in society seems to be fixed *a priori* and knows little variation. Difficulties are taken note of and sometimes improvements may even be brought about under persistent pressure, without, however, affecting the basic concept or introducing some constructive new thinking. Anyone slightly familiar with the Bible, where minorities and their lot are so often mentioned and where the fate of minorities is presented individually and collectively from the exodus of the Jews to the parable of the Good Samaritan (illustrated with examples of behavior), knows that this phenomenon is as old as history. But the fact that it is old and that one can already find examples in pre-biblical history should not discourage us or excuse us from trying to make a new start and to find new ways that may lead to a solution.

A look at the attempts and methods of the past makes one realize at once that in general it was only a choice between the ghetto and total integration. If, therefore, one was against the ghetto and apartheid, one had logically to opt for the complete abandonment of one's inheritance and achievement. Minorities were looked at, so to speak, as a passing stage which had to lead to either separation or fusion. When the American government, in one of its most generous actions concerned with immigration, accepted tens of thousands of Hungarian refugees from across the Atlantic in its operation "Safe Haven", it did so in spite of certain reservations made in the United States about Hungarian immigrants. They were—whether rightly or wrongly is beyond the present argument—accused of clinging too much to their national attitudes and of keeping Hungarian as a second language. One frequently met Hungarian-speaking Negroes, which at first sight proves the assertion, and therefore they did not become real Americans quickly enough.

The English attitude toward colored folk is somewhat different. People expect full integration, and therefore expect them to adjust themselves to laws and conventions, but they do not demand immediate total integration, partly because it is realized that they are dealing here with people with very ancient cultures, the value of which cannot be exclusively assessed in terms of what they contribute to the economy at present, and partly because they understand their own national formation, the labor of centuries, which cannot be achieved in one "biological moment" without doing harm. One could look on this attitude as a step toward that pluralism which is mentioned with increasing frequency in American literature.

Hence it is probable that in the future the United States, too, will no longer exact the total abandonment of national identities. It is even possible that one day the historical and national memories, until now only tolerated as decorative folklore, will be seen as enriching the new homeland. This is a bold concept, since up-to-date experiments seem to prove that complete assimilation is causing less trouble. But it is forgotten and overlooked here that the loss of identity, which outwardly often finds expression in a confrontation between generations, is a painful, damaging and gruesome process, beset with many disadvantages which are unnoticed only because what has here become disturbed, irrational and a source of irritation has become part of the gross national product. When there we meet wild behavior, uncertainty, short-term solutions, panic, lack of assimilation and a tendency toward crazy notions, it is no longer possible to find out what loss of what part of the inheritance lies at the root of any individual trouble.

If we could create at least stages that would lead to pluralism, much would have been achieved. It is true that pluralism as here indicated—and this would imply the acceptance of bilingual speech, as has been achieved in Yugoslavia (more precisely in the Slovenian-Hungarian border regions)—is but one possible way of tackling the national and minority problems more creatively than has so far been the case. But once a start has been made, one may imagine for once a chain reaction of something good. Love of neighbor is a supremely creative force; it must be released, given scope to operate and allowed to blossom into beauty.

Günter Struck/*Cologne, W. Germany*

The Modern
Sexual Revolution

Anyone who takes a casual walk through a large European city cannot help but notice the countless billboards, theater marquees and shop advertisements depicting the human figure in various stages of undress. The movie houses offer us "Frivolous Games" and "Forbidden Pleasures", an uncensored feast for the eyes. Racy literature, once buried in the dark corners of the bookstores, now fills the windows and the display racks.

But is this really the "sex wave" about which we have heard so much? When we talk about the sexual revolution, are we talking about the scantily clad girls that leap out at us from the covers of the slick magazines?

To answer "yes" to these questions is to overlook the full dimensions of this whole question. No one would seriously deny that there has been a greatly increased sexualization of public displays and advertising. But this is not true of advertising alone; intimate sexual relations have more and more become elements of public life. This basic phenomenon has deep roots in our whole anthropological background, and sociological and psychological factors are closely intertwined. The "sex wave" is an extremely complex phenomenon.

Some say that it is all a matter of business and profit. Others say that it is a question of artistic freedom. Still others assert that the phenomenon we are witnessing today is quite explicable in psychoanalytical terms. Be this as it may, the fact is that many people are unable to cope with the situation. There is hardly an adult who is totally uninfluenced by it—not to mention the child and the teenager.

Why the Sex Wave?

One might superficially describe this phenomenon as the public display of the human body, usually the female body, for the purpose of arousing certain emotions in the onlooker. Usually the body is not depicted "as God created it"; some clothing covers the primary and secondary sex characteristics. Quite frequently it is a matter of depicting the female form in provocative and exotic poses—on a rug, curled up in a chair, etc.

The publishers of the slick magazines will cite the profit motive as the reason for this emphasis on sex. Sales seem to be directly proportional to the provocative nature of the magazine's cover. The profit motive also seems to be the main reason behind sexy films.

Others take a different stand. They say that the present emphasis on sex is mainly a question of artistic expression. It ties in with the artistic sensitivities that are now shared by broader levels of society. For this reason, any attempt to introduce ethical or moral restrictions into the realm of art is staunchly opposed.

L. Marcuse[1] is a proponent of this position. He says that, in the interests of personal freedom, we have no right to oppose the representation of intimate human relations in the public sphere. He echoes the thoughts of many when he says: "As long as no one is forced to look, there is no reason for anyone to be scandalized. Those who enjoy looking should be able to; those who don't want to look don't have to."

In the juridical sphere, too, there are varying stances. B. R. Dünnwald, for example, says that artistic freedom should be absolute and not subject to the limits imposed on freedom of opinion

---

[1] L. Marcuse, "Kunst und Unzüchtigkeit," in *Juristische Rundschau* (1965), pp. 46ff.

and freedom of speech. In his opinion, it would be "ridiculous to lay down general, restrictive norms".[2]

When attempts are made to remove scandalous, unrestrainedly sexual representations from the public sphere, others rise in opposition in the name of artistic freedom.

But all this does not bring us to the heart of the problem. The fact is that countless numbers of people suffer from sexual problems. They have oppressed, or sublimated, or stultified their sexual life. For other people, sex has become a consumer product, a means of winning prestige or of satisfying infantile wishes and dreams.

On the other side of the coin, however, we must realize that sex has also become more real and human for many people. Having come to realize the deep inner relationship between body and soul, they have been able to integrate their sexual life into the framework of their total life and personality. The two sexes are able to meet each other more freely and to respect each other as persons.

What Does It Involve?

People give different answers to this question. Some talk about artistic expression. Others are scandalized about the whole trend and try desperately to counter it by legal measures. Still others see it as a reaction to the strict taboos of an older era. Undoubtedly such things are tied up with this question, but none of them are completely satisfying to one who tries to probe this problem in depth.

We must not forget that man, as a species, tends to fall under the sway of temporary fads and trends; fashions are a clear example of this. Behavioral scientists tell us that this trait is a relic of the herd mentality which man once had. Moreover, no one can deny that psychoanalysis and its findings has continued to play a part in the sex wave. In man we find certain drives and tensions that are below the level of consciousness. They

[2] Cf. H. G. Sellenthin, *Kunst in den Grenzen der Freiheit* (Cologne, 1967).

find expression in a wide variety of ways: artistic creation, work, sports, etc. But these drives do not necessarily lead to neuroses, as had once been assumed. Psychoanalysis now tells us that these drives and their emotional overtones can be resolved by being brought into the conscious realm. When these drives are reintroduced into consciousness through optical or acoustic experiences, the person can conquer the unconscious drives that have dominated him.

The question here is: What is being presented to the senses today? For the most part it would seem to be pictures and images of the female body, and one might be inclined to think that this is directed to the male population only. But that is not so. The psychological process of "identification" or "projection" must be taken into consideration. Many people unconsciously identify with the image that is presented to them. Women unconsciously identify with the girl who is in the stocking advertisement, and that is what the stocking firm is counting on, for their sales market is made up of women for the most part. To be sure, the man is affected by the ad too, but that will not find a direct echo in the sales figures.

In the book field, too, we can see the impact which sex has had on book sales. To mention but one example, there was Henry Miller's *Tropic of Cancer*. To play up the sex angle is to increase sales. Indeed, this takes on such proportions that pornography seems to be the only suitable word for it. Moreover, we now have nauseatingly detailed descriptions of all sorts of perverse scenes: homosexual and lesbian encounters, sado-masochistic activities, etc.

Herein lies the great danger in the present emphasis on sex. Sex life is being isolated from the life of the person as such; it is being treated as an isolated compartment. Man's erotic life is being depersonalized.

In his recent book,[3] H. Thielicke takes as his point of departure "the unity of *bios* and person in sexual activity". The present crisis is that this unity has been destroyed. Thielicke

[3] H. Thielicke, *Sex-Ethik der Geschlechtlichkeit* (Tübingen, 1966).

comments: "When sex becomes an indiscriminate activity, then man's nature as a person is threatened. . . . It would be erroneous to attribute the present decline in sexual mores to a decay in morals."

The fact that the decline in personal values has paralleled the decay in moral values in our day would seem to support this notion. Moreover, sex has become such an independent area that today it often does not relate to any partner, much less to the concrete image of a spouse.

In discussing the present situation, some people will point out that prostitution is on the decline. But whether this is a positive indicator is open to question. We do not find any significant increase in really close relationships between boy-girl couples as the cause of prostitution's decline. The number of people who have sex relations indiscriminately has actually increased, although the number of professional prostitutes may have declined. People may have affairs for days or weeks and then set out to look for new partners.

Dangers to Youth

The possible dangers in the new emphasis on sex cannot be spelled out fully. But there certainly are dangers involved, especially for young people. Young people, whose psychic growth does not keep pace with their physical growth, are brought face to face with sexual realities far too early in life. As a result, there is the danger that they will have deep misunderstandings about sex. They may come to regard the realm of sex and love as an isolated compartment, which need not and cannot be integrated into the total personality of the human being.

In countries where greater sexual freedom has existed for any length of time (e.g., Sweden and England), some of the consequences are already evident. The number of pregnant girls under 15 has risen sharply. More than likely, there has been a corresponding increase in the incidence of venereal disease.

M. Shofield draws a searing portrait of the tragic consequences of this rampant sexual atmosphere on young people. Yet he reaches an astonishing conclusion: "Despite all the influences at work on our young people—books, television, slick magazines, etc.—it would be wrong to regard our young people as a lazy, undisciplined generation obsessed with sex." [4]

In my opinion, his work is influenced by the same tendency which shows up in the report of the British Council of Churches.[5] This tendency is to accept prevailing patterns of behavior and to deal with them pragmatically by disseminating birth control information and warnings on venereal disease. In reading the report of the British Council of Churches, one is left with the indelible impression that one can no longer invoke objective moral standards. It suggests that "new developments have raised doubts about the notion of objective moral standards". As a result, "it is no longer a question of tying men and women to a fixed moral position on sexual morality; it is a question of instilling in them a characteristic personal attitude".

One would agree with this, insofar as a proper attitude toward sex must spring from a personal outlook. But a new appreciation of sexuality will only come from something that provides the basis for a corresponding pattern of conduct. It seems quite wrong to set up a contrast between "a fixed moral position on sexual morality" and "a characteristic personal attitude". This new dichotomy seems to be an attempt to come to terms with the moral pluralism of British society, which is composed of various social strata with different attitudes and behavior patterns in the area of sex.

Need for a New Catholic Approach

The critical question for Catholicism today is a meaningful pastoral approach to the sexual revolution. How can the Church and committed Christians tackle this burning issue? In general, we may say that the positive values of sex must be given deeper consideration. What is particularly needed is an integral personal

---

[4] M. Shofield, *The Sexual Behaviour of Young People* (London, 1965).
[5] *Sex and Morality* (London, 1966).

approach to the notion of purity and a revised approach to the establishment of concrete norms.

The laity is aware that some moral theologians (in Germany: Egenter, Auer, Weber, Böckle, Teichtweier) have long since taken note of the new outlook on man and his sexuality. In addition, men like J. Pieper, Dietrich von Hildebrand and Romano Guardini have spelled out a positive approach to the notion of purity.

Pieper describes the goal of purity as "unselfish self-possession". The pure person is the one who has integrated his sexual drives into his total personality. Any practicing psychotherapist can tell you how much distortion and confusion has existed in this area. For much too long a time, purity was identified with naïveté regarding sex.

Even today pastors of souls often equate purity with "custody of the senses". The body-soul, human-animal, dualism of Augustine has been bypassed on the theoretical level, but it is still at work in the area of actual practice. The senses are regarded with mistrust, and sensual life is regarded as somewhat less than good in itself. It is only recently that we have begun to realize the important and positive role of the sensual and the material in man's life. As R. Faber puts it: "Purity must involve the sensual life of man if it is not to become unnatural." [6]

No normal, healthy human being can disregard the power of the sex drive. Any attempt to flee its influence will bring neurosis and sickness in its wake. Purity does not require that we fear or flee the sex impulse; it requires, rather, that we educate and integrate our sexual impulses. Its goal is the harmonious integration of the sex drive into our total personality. The sex drive should put a distinctive and indelible stamp on the personality of man and woman. It is not something to be walled up; it is something which must be accorded its due place in the development of a full human life.

[6] F. R. Faber, "Keuschheit: Tugend oder Laster?" in *Unsere Seelsorge* (1966), pp. 16, 19.

When the sex drive is not properly integrated, when it is isolated from man's personality, then man's capacity for authentic love is undermined. If this is what real purity means, then impurity is the prevention of full self-development, the disruption of the process of developing our whole personality.

Lack of sex education is often cited as the cause of the sex explosion among young people, but this is incorrect. Any attempt at sex education, which is restricted to biological realities and processes, will prove abortive. To give our young people a proper appreciation of sex, we must provide them with the groundwork for sound sexual development; we must provide them not only with biological information, but also with the means to achieve full and integrated personal development.

Moreover, norms on sexual behavior must be provided as well. The question is: Where are we to derive the proper values and criteria? It would seem that much attention has been paid to this question by modern theologians (Doms, Fuchs, Auer, Böckle, David, Janssen). Both biblical history and Christian tradition bear witness to an impressive development of ethical norms regarding sexual behavior. One can certainly speak of "normative behavior" in this area.

Commenting on this tradition, Böckle says: "It is quite clear that these concrete norms are very much culturally conditioned, that they derive from a specific outlook on the whole issue." His conclusion is: "If Augustine, Thomas and other theologians were justified in laying down norms for Christian life on the basis of the contemporary outlook on sexuality, why should not today's theologians have the same right and the same duty? Such attempts should not be regarded as a desire to erase all norms or to avoid sacrifice." [7]

Today we are convinced that a proper understanding of human sexuality can only be derived from a personalist outlook. Every sphere of human activity must be understood and appreciated in human terms. Man certainly does possess a certain nature

---

[7] F. Böckle, "Sexualität und sittliche Norm," in *Stimmen der Zeit* (1967), pp. 180, 261.

that sets limits upon him and defines his possibilities. But it is a *human* nature. It is not the nature of a "ready-made" being; it is the nature of a "being that can be".

Man is not a being that is there, ready-made from the outset. He must become what he is by nature. "He must fashion his potentialities into a finished whole. He must make decisions and develop himself into the reality that he is. He does not toy despotically with his nature; he works out the potential imbedded in his nature. Man freely becomes what he is; that is the process tied up with human nature." [8]

Human sexuality, then, involves freedom; man gives meaning and shape to his sexual drive. Herein lies the great difference between human and animal sexuality. The latter is totally tied to instinct, so man's sex drive cannot be equated with this instinct-bound drive of animals. For the same reason, there is no need to pinpoint a generic sexual instinct in man and animals and then overlay this instinct with specifically human factors. The behavioral sciences have clearly shown us how different man is from brute animals.

Where do we go from there? Böckle puts it this way: "What we are dealing with is a fundamentally human relationship that is tied up with the duty of procreation. We must establish ethical guideposts for human sex relations which will relate this relationship to the culture and well-being of mankind as a whole. Various ethical systems could be considered in attempting to do this. From the Christian point of view, the basic law of love should serve as the foundation for this task. In other words, from the Christian viewpoint we must regard the relationship between man and woman as a summons to offer oneself to another, to find meaning and fulfillment in living for each other unceasingly." [9]

In a similar vein, A. Auer says: "The moral value of sexual activity is oriented to the personal value that finds expression

[8] J. B. Metz, "Natur," in *LThK* VII, col. 807.
[9] F. Böckle, *Geschlechtliche Beziehungen vor der Ehe* (Mainz, 1967), pp. 27f.

through it. This does not mean that some extraneous element is brought to bear on sexual activity, for sexual activity of itself is tied up with the integration of man's personality. The dynamism of sex is something which man must take cognizance of and develop. By expressing love through sexual activity, we come to a deeper knowledge of the other as a human person, and we help this person to fulfill himself or herself as such." [10]

One can only hope that the full implications of such insights will be explored as quickly as possible. In Vatican Council II's *Constitution on the Church in the Modern World,* the layman can hear echoes of different and differing positions. But, on the whole, we find an outlook on sex which could well serve as the basis for new directions in pastoral activity. Sexual love is accorded a value of its own. Sexual activity can no longer be tied solely to procreation, nor can it be subordinated to it. If we could get across these ideas to the men of our day, then we might be able to make a valuable contribution to the struggle against the sex wave. If we are to master the sex drive, we must integrate it into an outlook on marriage and love that will reveal its truly human quality.

[10] A. Auer, in *Handbuch Theol. Grundbegr.* I (Munich, 1963), p. 500.

Franz Furger / *Lucerne, Switzerland*

Prudence and Moral Change

The gradual development which pervades our modern age has made modern man not only more conscious of change in general but has also given him a deeper understanding of the way things have developed—i.e., of the historicity of all that is human, and hence also of the institutions and norms that appeared to be fixed for all times. Moral theology, which Sertillange defined as "the science of what man should be, based on what man is", will therefore interpret this being of man not as something static and essentially supratemporal, but as something historical, and therefore changeable and dynamic; it will have to draw the consequences of this situation for the norms of morality.

The general theme of this volume, as well as of the individual contributions which try to find practical norms for a Christian attitude toward the burning issues of our society, shows that we are looking for an adjustment to the changed situation. However, there is still the question of whether this new opening toward a dynamic understanding can be achieved by a simple break with the prevailing traditional teaching up until now or whether this can be done as a no doubt new, yet legitimate development. Insofar as the concrete solution of contemporary moral problems is concerned, this linking up with tradition is of course actually only of secondary importance; yet, within the historical understanding of doctrine, it demands an explanation. Moreover, such a connection between the present and past of moral theology might help to overcome the uncertainty of many people who, fearing the danger of sheer novelties, feel antagonistic toward any development in teaching.

A Brief Look at History

In the classical teaching of Aristotelian Thomism, the task of coordinating and applying moral conduct to the concrete circumstances of life fell under the heading of prudence as the most important of all cardinal virtues. It would appear therefore that we should look there for the connection between the problems of today and tradition. It is true that, in spite of the confrontation between the cyclical thinking of antiquity and the eminently historical message of Christian salvation, a proper understanding of historical development escaped both antiquity and the Middle Ages. Thus one can hardly expect that we shall find there a conscious understanding of prudence as an historical virtue. Nevertheless, the changeableness of a human nature which is essentially bound up with finitude and temporal conditions remains at least open in principle with regard to this virtue. Unfortunately, this openness to change was lost at the beginning of the modern age with its inclination toward rational clarity and straightforward deductions. The prevailing casuistry that situated every individual situation logically under general laws was blind to historical change and the creative moment contained in that change. The only sense in which the so-called *Mirrors for Princes* (*Fürstenspiegel*), written for the education of the political elite, and the occasional spiritual writings preserved the sense of the originality of human actions lay in the application of prudence to the constantly changing circumstances of life. And so the treatise on prudence, which occupied a key position in earlier ages, disappeared significantly and increasingly from current manuals.

Nevertheless, in the controversy about the validity of the various "moral systems" concerned with the solution of cases of conscience and combining fixed laws with concrete situations, what was formerly the concern of prudence was at least not wholly forgotten. In any case, when these moral systems have to be explained today, there is usually a return to this prudence which was formerly the central virtue.

This article seeks to provide an outline of this process, and in doing so we shall work in the direction of a newly formulated demand [1]—not merely a retrospective understanding but an historical, dynamic and creative understanding which looks toward the future.

The Neo-Thomist Return to the Treatise on Prudence

This return to the function of prudence in Catholic moral theology did not take place in a dialogue with the problems of a changing society, but arose out of a general reassessment of medieval thought in Neo-Thomism. The most explicit, though not the first,[2] demand for emphasis on the function of prudence in moral theology was made by T. Deman.[3] Constantly referring to the teaching of St. Thomas, he sharply opposed that balancing of opinions of authors as it was generally practiced in the various systems, particularly in that of probabilism. For the moral human act is not determined by the view of this or that moral theologian on the degree of validity of a positive law in a concrete instance, but only by the *circumstantial situation* itself. This determination follows from the unalterable moral principles of the original conscience (the so-called "synderesis"), but as soon as these principles are brought into play for application; therefore, since these principles necessarily lose something of their universality under the pressure of the constantly changing situation, they fall under the influence of that mistress of all virtues, prudence.[4]

---

[1] Cf. I. Lobo, "Toward a Morality Based on the Meaning of History," in *Concilium* 25 (1967), pp. 23–46.

[2] The first was probably H. D. Noble in "La Prudence" in the French edition of *Summa theol.*, II–II 47–56 (Paris, 1925).

[3] T. Deman, "Probabilisme," in *DThC* XIII/1, cols. 419–619 (1936).

[4] This brief summary is based on T. Deman, *Aux origines de la théologie morale* (Paris, 1951), esp. pp. 108f.

After such basic statements, one rightly wants to see this function of prudence described in greater detail, and one would expect to discover its creative element with regard to moral conduct in a changing society. Unfortunately, the moment for such a discovery does not seem to have yet been reached. Deman does not place the guarantee of objectivity and truth in a fresh appreciation of the concrete situation in the light of the general principles, but in the moral law as such, which prudence knows about and which it applies unconditionally. This is a basic "tutiorism" (system which inclines toward what is safer), which Deman has not given up even in his later writings.[5]

R. Garrigou-Lagrange[6] and H. D. Noble[7] also refer to St. Thomas for greater stress on prudence in the establishing of moral (i.e., practical) truth. But prudence is here again more differentiated as the virtue which makes us strive after a fixed end. Noble defines this aim still more precisely as simply "the good", so that prudence as the striving after an aim coincides with the readiness to subordinate oneself constantly to the will of God.[8] In spite of this useful opening, the discussion remains almost totally limited to the question of the applicability of positive moral law to a complex situation.[9] Moreover, as soon as one turns away, however slightly, from a "tutiorism" like that of Deman, the very formal formulation of these more far-reaching attempts makes one suspect that they hide some kind of subjectivism. Thus H. M. Héring's[10] statement that according to St. Thomas natural law allows of exceptions *in paucioribus,* and

[5] Cf. the 2nd edition of *La prudence* (see note 2) by Deman (1949).

[6] Cf. R. Garrigou-Lagrange, "Du caractère métaphysique de la théologie morale (en particulier dans les rapports de la prudence et de la conscience)," in *Rev. Thom.* 30 (1925), pp. 341–55; *idem,* "La prudence et la vie intérieure," in *VS* 51 (1937), pp. 24–41; *idem,* "La prudence, sa place dans l'organisme des vertus," in *Rev. Thom.* 31 (1926), pp. 411–26.

[7] Apart from Noble's commentary (note 2), see his *Le discernement de la conscience* (Paris, 1934).

[8] Noble, *op. cit.* (note 2), p. 89.

[9] Cf. the publications by P. Lumbreras, J. Tonneau and M. Labourdette.

[10] H. M. Héring, "Quomodo solvendi sunt casus: recurrenda ad sola principia an etiam ad prudentiam," in *Angelicum* 28 (1941), pp. 311–45.

therefore in some definite particular cases, needs qualification. At the time of his writing (his essay appeared in 1941), when under the pretext of such exceptions the most elementary dignity of man was trampled underfoot in Europe, such statements were bound to provoke a reaction.

This reaction came very soon from the pen of G. Gundlach[11] who wanted to see prudence formally described as striving after an aim complemented by the material norm of man's personal dignity as a spiritual, yet finite element—i.e., tending toward and conditioned by the absolute.[12] This would link the subjective intention with an objective scale of values, and both would constitute genuine morality through prudence, as was worked out by D. Capone, a disciple of Gundlach's, in a little-known thesis which appeared at that time.[13]

In spite of this somewhat fierce discussion among the theologians, the whole problematic remained rather theoretical and academic. It needed an outside impulse to become concrete and real. This soon came about through the rise of the strongly subjective "situation ethics" which queried the whole complex of traditional norms in general.

Pius XII and "Situation Ethics"

While this new movement in morality remained rather confined to professional authors in Germany, mainly among evangelical theologians (following Kierkegaard, particularly E. Griesebach, E. Thurneysen and Karl Barth), but also among some Catholics like B. E. Michel,[14] in France it combined during the first years after the war with the then popular existentialist philosophy, particularly of J.-P. Sartre and A. Camus, and thus affected large circles of young Catholics.[15] In these circum-

[11] G. Gundlach, "Klugheit als Prinzip des Handelns," in *Gr* 23 (1942), pp. 238–54.

[12] Cf. his explanation of "rectitudo appetitus", *ibid.,* pp. 247f.

[13] D. Capone, *Intorno alla verità morale* (Naples, 1951).

[14] Cf. several articles by M. Galli in *Orient.* 14 (1950).

[15] Cf. the memorandum addressed by the *Weltbund weiblicher kath. Jugend* to Pius XII, to which the pope refers explicitly in his address of April 24, 1952 (*AAS* 44 [1952], p. 414).

stances the Church authorities, and finally Pope Pius XII, thought they could no longer remain silent. In two addresses and an instruction from the Holy Office, the pope defined his attitude toward these relativist tendencies in morality.[16]

In this context, however, we are less interested in the condemnation of the relativism that this understanding of ethics seemed to imply than in the reference to the classical teaching on prudence which "contains all that is good and positive in situation ethics without its errors and deviations".[17] Although this remark is not the keynote of the papal statements, we owe it to this observation that, in spite of the pope's rejection of situation ethics in Catholic moral theology, the necessary research and discussion about the central issues of this new tendency could carry on. It can hardly be doubted that the preceding theoretical debate about the importance of prudence contributed to this possibility, and that was its merit.

Among the earliest commentaries, even those that were most opposed to this new morality maintained this possibility of a certain understanding,[18] and the articles by J. Fuchs were particularly impressive.[19] Here we have, for the first time as far as I know, and almost casually (in a footnote), a reference to a twofold understanding of the prudent application of general norms to concrete situations:[20] there is first of all the deduction which may be satisfactory for an individual case in peaceful times, and may therefore guarantee a "morality for short periods

[16] Addresses of March 23 and April 24 in *AAS* 44 (1952), pp. 270–78 and 413–19; *Instr. S. Off.*, Feb. 2, 1956 (*AAS* 48), pp. 144–45.

[17] *AAS* 44 (1952), p. 418, with ref. to *Summa theol.* II–II. 47–56.

[18] Cf. F. Hürth, "Kommentare zu den päpstlichen Ansprachen von 1952," in *Per. RMCL* 41 (1952), pp. 223–49; *idem,* "On the Instruction of 1956," in *Per. RMCL* 45 (1956), pp. 140–204.

[19] J. Fuchs, "Morale théologique et morale de situation," in *NRTh* 76 (1954), pp. 1073–85, and "Ethique objective et éthique de situation (à propos de l'instruction du Saint Office du 2 fév., 1956)," in *NRTh* 78 (1956), pp. 798–818; cf. the less qualified but basically identical interpretation in J. Kraus, "Sittliche Existenz als Massstab des praktisch Wahren (vom berechtigten Anliegen der Situationsethik)," in *LS* 9 (1958), pp. 60–68.

[20] J. Fuchs, "Ethique . . . ," *op. cit.,* p. 804, note 11.

of time", and then there is the second way which, while following general directives, understood here as the expression of ontological structures, creates a new original solution in view of the concrete and even unique situation and thus leads to a "morality of the *kairos*", of the moment of absolute originality.[21]

This opens the way toward understanding the real concern of situation ethics (namely, the right time of the moral decision, personal commitment, honesty without legalism, etc.) and securing a place for it in principle, even in Catholic moral theology. In spite of the justified reference to prudence as the virtue which embraces precisely these features, the question remains what the dynamic force may be which in this creative phase leads to the discovery of new solutions.

Situation Ethics in Moral Theology

Here all that has been done in recent years to renew moral theology should be mentioned since it all contributed something toward the process of extricating moral teaching from a petrified casuistic legalism and inspiring it with a new dynamism for the present "kairos", the new and decisive present. One may think here of the work done by F. Tillmann and R. Hofmann on the "imitation of Christ" as the key to moral truth. One thought seems to have been of particular importance—in fact, closely aligned with the main theme behind the "imitation of Christ"—because it concentrates directly and formally on this dynamic force itself; moreover, Noble's and Garrigou-Lagrange's views on prudence as the striving after the absolute good has some bearing on this. I refer to the stress on charity as the formative principle of all virtues according to tradition, as shown in the work of R. Carpentier and G. Gilleman.[22] Although Gilleman mentions prudence as a morally creative virtue only briefly and Carpentier nowhere mentions it explicitly, the context of their work makes it

---

[21] These expressions are taken from I. Lobo (*op. cit.*).

[22] R. Carpentier, "Conscience," in *DSp* II (Paris, 1953), cols. 1548–75; G. Gilleman, *Le primat de la charité en théologie morale* (Paris/Tournai, [2]1954).

clear that, on the one hand, prudence situates the trivialities of every day in the all-embracing dynamism of love,[23] while, on the other, it helps, when in doubt, to get beyond the rigid law and, as a genuine form of *epikeia* (the taking of a personal decision by one's own light), to find the concrete will of God in that source of law which is God himself, and therefore in love and goodness.[24] This not only does justice to the modern demand that purpose and intention should be respected in moral conduct, but this purpose finds here that transcendental and hence truly dynamic adjustment which alone makes a creative commitment possible.

It is hardly astonishing that this view found much support. C. A. J. van Ouwerkerk[25] and C. Nink[26] linked it explicitly with the traditional teaching on prudence. It spread through more broadly based manuals, such as those of O. Lottin[27] and J. Fuchs,[28] while recently this view was again more emphatically connected with Aquinas by W. Kluxen.[29] However new this view may appear as it arose through contact with situation ethics, all this work shows how closely it approaches the best elements of tradition and even interprets this tradition in authentic fashion for our time. Whether prudence is explicitly mentioned or not (as in Carpentier) is of course unimportant.

In spite of all this, there is still no proper synthesis of these

---

[23] Cf. Gilleman, *op. cit.,* pp. 190f.

[24] Carpentier has declared that he agrees with this interpretation of his article on conscience, while stressing that prudence must never be understood as merely acquired, but also as a grace (cf. the review of F. Furger's *Gewissen und Klugheit* (Luzern, 1965) in *NRTh* 98 (1966), pp. 548–49.

[25] C. A. J. van Ouwerkerk, *Caritas et Ratio. Etude sur le double principe de la vie morale d'après S. Thomas d'Aquin* (Nijmegen, 1956).

[26] C. Nink, *Metaphysik des sittlichen Guten* (Freiburg i. B., 1955).

[27] O. Lottin, *Principes de morale,* 2 vols. (Louvain, 1947); *idem, Morale fondamentale* (Paris, 1954).

[28] J. Fuchs, *Theologia moralis fundamentalis,* Part I (Rome, 1960), and his expanded version of *lex naturae* in *Le droit naturel. Essai théologique* (Paris, 1960).

[29] W. Kluxen, *Philosophische Ethik bei Thomas von Aquin* (Mainz, 1964), esp. pp. 221f.

new insights which would allow us to see how prudence can trace in the concrete facts of a situation that path which will lead to a decision that is truly concordant with love. Here a substantial contribution was made by Karl Rahner.

Rahner's "Existential Ethics" as a Possible Synthesis

A glance at Rahner's rich work[30] shows that he is keenly interested in the problems created by situation ethics. He seems to have been less directly concerned here with moral theology than with the approach of existentialist philosophy. As with Kierkegaard and Heidegger, the common root seemed to suggest an immediate analogy between our question and the question of personal and individual self-realization. Rahner himself stresses that what his existential ethics has in common with every kind of situation ethics is the emphasis on the fact that "there is a moral individuality (*individuum*) of a positive kind which cannot be fitted into a simple general ethics; there is something unique which is nevertheless morally binding".[31] By "human person" Rahner means "a being that makes his own decisions freely within his nature (i.e., the whole complex of all the conditioning elements, grace included, which make up his humanity)";[32] hence a simple deduction from general norms is inadequate when a person has to make a truly original moral decision.

Therefore, when we have to discover the always personal "imperative" in the general "principles",[33] only the second method, the inductive one, as mentioned by Fuchs, can be of any use in the application of general principles. Rahner's thought, which he likes to describe as existential ethics in contrast with the relativist

[30] K. Rahner, particularly in "Ueber die Fragen einer fundamentalen Existential-ethik," in *Schriften II* (Einsiedeln, ²1956), pp. 227–46 and *Das Dynamische in der Kirche* (Freiburg i. B., 1958).

[31] K. Rahner, "Ueber die Fragen . . . ," *op. cit.,* pp. 239–40.

[32] For the notion of "person" in Rahner, see F. Böckle, "Bestrebungen in der Moraltheologie heute," in *Fragen der Theologie heute* (Einsiedeln, 1957), pp. 431–35.

[33] These concepts are explained in detail in "Prinzipien und Imperative," in *Das Dynamische . . . , op. cit.,* pp. 14–37.

situation ethics, made a double contribution. First of all, this approach is more than simply another, more practical method; it is integrated in a whole anthropological and ontological image of man where "nature" and the ungraspable "individuality" are both seen as constitutive of the full personality and hence belong to the person's morality. Second, Rahner adds an important precision in that this wholly personal imperative includes not only the natural elements but also the call of God's grace which man experiences in his concrete situation and which must be understood as such. According to Rahner, this specific insight is due to prudence which is here understood as both naturally acquired and as a gift of the Spirit. Therefore it becomes, so to speak, a kind of flair for what God wants me to do precisely here and now.

Within the general ethical structure this view recognizes the always concrete solution as both a theoretical speculative truth and as the clear demand, directed to me personally, of "thou shalt" (i.e., a practical truth, although the two usually can only be understood by the analyzing mind).[34] This comprehensive function of prudence, involving both mind and will, was already elaborated in the Middle Ages, and this was not overlooked in the earlier stages of the new thinking about this virtue (especially in O. Lottin and D. Capone), but only Rahner made it so obvious and so free from mere theoretical classification.

This analysis also enabled Rahner to describe prudence in more practical detail, for we still have to explain how I can understand a given possible decision as binding on me. For this Rahner refers to the "considerations of choice" and the "rules for the discernment of the spirits" in the *Exercises of St. Ignatius of Loyola*,[35] and he does so under the significant title of *The Logic of Existential Knowledge in Ignatius*.[36] He is here particularly interested in the so-called "second period of choice" (*Wahlzeit*), where "much clarity and insight can be gained from

---

[34] *Ibid.*, p. 93.
[35] In the *Exercises of St. Ignatius,* nn. 169–89 and 314–36.
[36] Cf. *Das Dynamische* . . . , *op. cit.,* p. 74.

the experience of consolation and disappointment",[37] and where, therefore, clarity does not arise from mere rational reflection or from mystical visions but must normally be looked for with prudence. Assuming the basic will to serve God and the consequent control of the discovered solution by means of the basic structures of morality, the criteria of Ignatius' rules of discernment (e.g., inner calm, balance and cheerfulness or uncertainty and nervousness at the evaluation of the various possible decisions) will suggest which one applies to my case. These inner situations of "consolation" must be understood as indications of whether the appropriate choice conforms with that basic dynamism of love which determines the life of a Christian and which tries to find God in all things in order to fulfill his will. This finding of God in all things is but the permanent practice of that supernatural existential logic which finds the will of God in the experience of the consolation where "through the frequent confrontation of the object of the choice with the basic consolation, one's experience tells whether these phenomena are inwardly harmonious and fit in with each other, and whether the will, concerned with this choice, maintains and increases or weakens and obscures that openness toward God in the experience of supernatural transcendence".[38]

These words of Rahner make it more clear than long explanations would that we are dealing in these at first rather strange "spiritual exercises" with genuine forms of prudence which must be constantly acquired or given anew as an intellectual and moral virtue, and which must ensure a perfect realization of the human person in his whole being as an individual and as related to the community.

And so these thoughts of Karl Rahner show how the concern of situation ethics can be actually worked out in Catholic moral theology through a deepened understanding of the traditional teaching on prudence; thus, without the danger of a subjective

[37] *Exercises*, n. 176.
[38] *Das Dynamische* . . . , *op. cit.*, pp. 135 and 138.

individualism, a genuine individual and personal ethics is possible as "existential ethics".

Further Problems

Insofar as the issues brought up by existentialism and situation ethics concerned the individual human person, an answer could be found in the framework of moral theology. But today we are confronted with increasingly urgent social problems. The recognition of "the signs of the times", stressed by John XXIII and Paul VI in their important encyclicals[39] and by Vatican Council II in its *Constitution on the Church in the Modern World,* is not so much concerned with individual morality (such as personal vocation, etc.) but almost exclusively with the burning social issues of our age. The individual moral attitude is only mentioned insofar as it contributes toward or hampers the solution of these problems.

Has prudence anything to contribute here? Once again, the beginning of an answer can be found in tradition. For the old Greeks this virtue was primarily related to the community and was essentially a "political virtue", particularly necessary in rulers. Insofar as antiquity and the Middle Ages thought in terms of monarchy or aristocracy (and had to do so, given the general level of civilized society), this included in principle the care for the welfare of the community. However, when we look for the social components of prudence in modern literature, this point of view seems to be almost completely absent.

Therefore, we need a corresponding deeper reflection on this point. Here it is not particularly difficult to apply the old principles of political prudence to the active politician of today. As the most important elements of such modern political prudence, one might mention, on the basis of unswerving respect for the personal dignity of man and love of neighbor in general: constancy in the matter of principles and elasticity, exact information and

[39] Cf. Pope John's *Mater et Magistra* (1961) and *Pacem in terris* (1963); Pope Paul's *Ecclesiam suam* (1964) and *Populorum progressio* (1967).

the courage of one's own conviction, perseverance in what is essential and flexibility in matters of secondary importance, and a certain elegance in social intercourse.[40]

But this is far from all. We are living in an increasingly democratic society where everyone, not only the expert and the professional politician, is responsible for the community. Moreover, our society is by no means going through a period of peace but rather through a period of breathtaking change with all the problems this implies (e.g., industrialization marked by automation, a unification of the technical world in spite of all social contrasts, etc.). Here the individual person can, and as a Christian must, contribute to a solution worthy of man through his individual attitude, his example and the possible political (i.e., public) expression of his opinion. How else can this be done except through the basic virtue of prudence which, apart from natural ability, must be inspired by the dynamism of charity, that Christian love of neighbor, without which there is ultimately no love of God either? Whether this is not really meant by that "emancipation", so often mentioned today and so urgently demanded of the modern Christian, is a matter that is still to be investigated.[41] The name is not important here. But I hope that these reflections have shown that it must be the spirit of what once was described as prudence, the "guide of all the virtues", which must lead toward a solution of the problems discussed in this volume.

[40] Cf. F. Furger, "Politik und christliche Klugheit," in *Civitas* 23.

[41] Cf. A. Sustar, "Was heisst eigentlich ein mündiger Laie?" in *Civitas* 23, pp. 127–38. For a more extensive bibliography, see F. Furger, *Gewissen und Klugheit* (Luzern, 1965), pp. 183–88.

PART II
BIBLIOGRAPHICAL
SURVEY

Jean-Paul Lichtenberg, O.P./*Strasbourg, France*

Strength and Weakness of the Declaration on the Jews

After having given us the echo of "Catholic and Protestant Comment on the Council Declaration on the Jews",[1] Msgr. John Oesterreicher presents us with some "Jewish Comments on the Conciliar Statement". Everyone will be grateful to the head of the Institute of Judaeo-Christian Studies of Seton Hall University for thus providing the reader with a first-class collection of the statements and reactions provoked by the publication of so important a document.

Since we ourselves have had occasion to present and comment on the conciliar Declaration on the Jews,[2] we would like to add to Msgr. Oesterreicher's two articles in *Concilium* a few points of comment and, perhaps, of disagreement.

To our mind, the overall impression given by these articles is that, taken all in all, the present definitive document *Nostra aetate,* setting the schema on the Jews within the wider setting of all non-Christian religions, is conclusively satisfactory. It is true, of course, that Msgr. Oesterreicher does justice to the criticisms, whether from the Christian or the Jewish point of view, by his recognition of certain omissions or clumsinesses in

---

[1] *Concilium* 24, pp. 127–42; 28, pp. 91–102.

[2] J.-P. Lichtenberg, "Contenu et portée de la Déclaration conciliare sur les Juifs," in *Nouv. Rev. Théol.* 3 (1966), pp. 225–48; *L'Eglise et les religions non-chrétiennes, presentation, traduction et commentaire de la déclaration "Nostra Aetate"* (Mulhouse/Paris/Tournai, 1967).

the final drafting of the document. But more than once he appears reluctant to admit the weakness or the negative side of the Declaration on the Jews, a fact easily understood when it is remembered that he personally worked on its drafting. Nevertheless, the limitations of this text are glaringly obvious when one compares it, for example, to the version of November 24, 1964, in which was found the demand: "That the Jewish people should never be presented as a race accursed or reprobate or *guilty of deicide*", and in which was the statement: "The Council . . . deplores and *condemns* (*damnat*) the hatred and persecutions of which the Jews have been the victims. . . ."

Since everything, or very nearly everything, has already been said [3] on the circumstances and motives which led the Secretariat for Unity to modify substantially, and from session to session, the projected *Decretum de Judaeis* that Cardinal Bea had been especially deputed to prepare, we shall not here delay on this aspect of the question. Our intention is rather to show simultaneously both sides of the coin, the strength and the weakness of this important document, in order to be able thereafter to establish a few signposts on the path of Judaeo-Christian dialogue, since that dialogue is the ultimate purpose of Vatican Council II's Declaration on the Jews. Our ideas will follow the lines of the three features which, to our mind, characterize the document on the Jews, taken as a whole: its insertion within the wider context of the non-Christian religions; the fact, so far as the Church is concerned, of a revision of the Christian viewpoint and attitude with regard to the Jewish people; the proposal made by the Church for a dialogue with Israel. As we deal with each of these, we shall bring out its two aspects, negative and positive.

[3] Cf. Y. Congar, *Le Concile au jour le jour, 4e Session* (Paris, 1966), pp. 155–67; A. Bea, *L'Eglise et le Peuple Juif* (Paris, 1967), pp. 21–26, 171–75; R. Laurentin, *L'Eglise et les Juifs à Vatican II* (Paris, 1967), *passim.*

I

THE INSERTION OF THE DOCUMENT ON THE JEWS
WITHIN THE WIDER CONTEXT OF THE NON-CHRISTIAN RELIGIONS

1. *The Advantages*

The emotional climate, the disputes and the bargaining process that formed the setting for the Declaration on the Jews, from its inception to its completion, will at least have succeeded in placing reflection concerning the Jewish people within the wider setting of reflection on the non-Christian religions. Something not at all foreseen at the beginning came into existence *de facto* thanks to a kind of salutary competition. It was around the Declaration on the Jews that the texts concerning the non-Christian religions gradually gathered, somewhat in the way of iron filings attracted by a magnet. "The progressive expansion of the *Decretum de Judaeis* into the *Declaration on Non-Christian Religions,* taken as a whole, was an undeniable enrichment." [4] When Cardinal Bea presented the final version of the text to the conciliar assembly on November 20, 1964, he was right to compare the Declaration to the grain of mustard seed that becomes a tree, according to the parable: "With the passing of time, and above all in consequence of the discussions that have taken place in this aula, this grain has, thanks to you, become almost a tree in whose branches many birds have already built their nests. In a certain sense all non-Christian religions . . . have their place in it." [5]

This widening of perspectives also led the editors to furnish a Preface that underlines the phenomenon of the unification of the modern world by the development of bonds and relationships between men and peoples, and to bring the document to an end with a conclusion which, asserting the universal brotherhood of all men in Christ, excludes every sort of discrimination. Taken as a whole, therefore, the *Declaration on the Relationship of the Church to Non-Christian Religions* acquired a scale proportionate

[4] R. Laurentin, *op. cit.,* p. 28.
[5] A. Bea, *op. cit.,* p. 166.

to the non-Christian religious world, a fact at which one can only rejoice.

2. The Disadvantages

Everyone knows that the schema on the Jews, in the course of its dramatic and eventful history, was intended for a whole series of different contexts. It was first of all envisaged within the framework of *De oecumenismo,* then as an appendix to *De Ecclesia;* it was also for a moment attached to the *Decree on Religious Freedom,* and ended up suspended in the void as an independent text.[6] It is now inserted within the framework of the document on non-Christian religions but one can legitimately ask if that is really where it belongs.

If the intention was to speak of the Jewish religion in this document (and we shall see further on that there was no such intention), a first disadvanatge is immediately apparent—namely that the Jewish religion, a revealed religion according to the tradition of the Church, has been placed on the same level as non-revealed religions. With that professional accuracy for which he is well known, Yves Congar has put his finger on this defect: "If the theme of the People of God had been treated *historically* in the conciliar *Constitution on the Church, that* would have been the place at which to speak of the Jewish people." [7] However, it is dealt with but very briefly in *Lumen gentium* (nn. 9 and 16).

Another place at which to speak of the Jewish people would have been in the *Decree on Ecumenism,* since the question of Israel is found both at the point of departure and at the destination of the unity of the People of God, if we look at the problem from the standpoint of St. Paul in the Epistle to the Romans. Our document did not have the good luck to win an entry here, and that is a great pity. However, "hunted from place to place, the

---

[6] Cf. R. Laurentin, *op. cit.,* for the history of this document.

[7] Y. Congar, *op. cit.,* p. 158; F. Lovsky, "La Déclaration sur les relations de l'Eglise avec les religions non-chrétiennes," in *Vatican II, points de vue de théologiens protestants* (Paris, 1967), pp. 149–69. Lovsky criticizes the Declaration on this precise point on pp. 152–53.

original Decree *De Judaeis* provoked reflection and bore fruit wherever it went".[8] Since the Declaration is only the first stage of a process, it is to be hoped that theological reflection on this subject will go on within the Secretariat for Unity, which has reserved the Jewish question for itself.

Another more serious disadvantage is this: Can it really be said that the document on the Jews, forming Chapter 4 of the Declaration *Nostra aetate,* is dealing with the "Jewish religion"? In spite of the fact that this title was proposed by the Secretariat for Unity in the various official translations of the Latin text, there is room for doubt. It is perfectly true that this text speaks of the "descendants of Abraham", of the "people" of the "old Alliance", of the "Jews" or of the "Jewish people", but it nowhere mentions the "religio Judaica" or "Mosaica" or even the word "Judaismus" which one might have expected. There is no doubt that the text deals with "the Jewish people", its vocation and its religious destiny, but not with Judaism as a *religion*. It would therefore have been better to give this fourth chapter of the Declaration the title of "The Jewish People". However, when one remembers the insurmountable difficulties raised by the bishops of the Middle East, against which the Declaration on the Jews had to make its way, one will not be too tempted to blame the editors for softening the blow and getting out of the underlying political difficulties by the use of the title "The Jewish Religion".

That having been said, one is still justified in asking whether the editors had a very clear view of the Jewish question under its contemporary religious aspect. Judaism is, after all, a complex reality that simultaneously embraces the Jewish people and the Jewish religion. The confusion of the two components of Judaism, namely, the nation and the religion, made it difficult, in fact impossible, to treat of "the Jewish religion" in isolation. If the intention was to speak of that, then the text should have spoken of Judaism *as a religion* and recognized its values, its contemporary relevance and its mission in the world of today. But the

[8] R. Laurentin, *op. cit.,* p. 28.

text we have manifestly has nothing like this approach to the question. It is content to recall everything that Christianity owes to the Jewish people and what the Church thinks of her relationship with it. This is a little brief. One day, therefore, the question will have to be tackled again from a different direction if a Christian theology of Judaism is to be worked out.

II

A REVISION OF THE CHRISTIAN VIEWPOINT AND ATTITUDE
WITH REGARD TO THE JEWISH PEOPLE

Presenting once again the dossier of Christian anti-Semitism which the Jewish historian J. Isaac had characterized as "an education in contempt", the agnostic Jewish sociologist G. Friedmann, in his absorbing work *Fin du Peuple Juif?*, summoned the Catholic Church to an "agonizing reappraisal": "If the third session of the Council takes the road of such evasions, such 'raison d'Eglise' and such compromises as motivated the silence of Pius XII, then Catholicism will have missed a magnificent opportunity to make the Great Revision of its attitude with regard to Judaism." [9]

At the end of the fourth session, the Council did have the courage to make this "Great Revision" by maintaining in the final text a position which implicitly condemns anti-Semitism and declares the Jewish people not guilty of the sin of deicide.

1. *The Magnitude of This Revision*

As has been said, this revision is to be found in the assertion of formulas quite strong enough to eliminate "every form of anti-Semitism" and to correct a view, falsely called "traditional", of the trial and death of Christ. We have developed elsewhere[10] the implications, as regards both doctrine and practice, of this new appraisal by the Church of the Jewish people's part in the con-

---

[9] G. Friedmann, *Fin du Peuple Juif?* (Paris, 1965), p. 309.
[10] J. P. Lichtenberg, *op. cit.,* in *Nouv. Rev. Théol.* 3 (1966), pp. 225–48.

demnation and trial of Jesus of Nazareth. Let us sum it up in the statement that the present text of the Declaration rejects the position of those who consider that the Jewish people, rendering itself guilty of the crime of deicide against the person of Christ, can be considered "rejected" and "accursed" by God. The document thereafter invites those responsible for Christian catechesis "to teach nothing that is incompatible with the truth of the Gospel and the spirit of Christ"; it "condemns" and "deplores", finally, "the persecutions and manifestations of anti-Semitism which, of whatever era and authorship, have been directed against the Jews".

The importance of this revision did not escape the president of the World Jewish Congress, Nahum Goldmann, who on the day after the text's promulgation proclaimed that the Declaration "eliminates the age-old accusation of deicide . . . which formed the basis of numberless persecutions and cruel injustices committed by the Catholic Church against the Jewish people" (*Le Monde* 20 [1965], p. 10).

It is by another reappraisal that the Council, "gazing into the depths of the mystery of the Church", has rediscovered the profound historical and mystical bonds that unite the Jewish people to the Christian people.[11] This obviously is not, properly speaking, a *new* truth for the Church, but if a certain number of ancient official documents[12] are compared with that of Vatican Council II, one is struck by the new tone of the *Declaration on the Non-Christian Religions* in general and on the Jews in particular. To paraphrase Cardinal König, one might say that this is "the first time in the history of the Church that a Council has in this way devoted itself" to the Jewish question.

2. *The Limitations of This Revision*

The limitations are glaringly obvious as soon as one parallels the two versions of the text presented to the assembly, the first

[11] Cf. P. Beauchamp, "L'Eglise et le Peuple Juif," in *Etudes* 7 (1964); J. Hoffmann, "Vatican II et les Juifs," in *Esprit* 7 (1966), pp. 1155ff.

[12] R. Laurentin, *op. cit.,* pp. 16–20.

on November 24, 1964 and the second on October 28, 1965. The latter and definitive version omits any mention of the word "deicide" and no longer "condemns" but only "deplores" the manifestations of anti-Semitism.

No man has more strongly underlined the weaknesses of this final version than Abbé René Laurentin: "Let us suppose that persecutions of the Jews cease forever, or that at least they no longer find among Christians either sympathizers or accomplices, in spite of all that has happened in the last 1,500 years; then the process of diminution suffered by the text, above all the suppression of the clause on deicide, will have been no more than a last and unimportant incident. But let us suppose, on the contrary, that the endless recurrence of the same factors of historical determinism brings about new persecutions, a new genocide, then mankind would judge harshly this decision to incur the risk involved in the failure to tear out more thoroughly the emotional roots of anti-Semitism; they would judge it as one of those historical faults from which the Church is not immune, as is clearly shown by certain episodes in her history." [13]

Even graver, for purposes of catechetical revision, is the disappearance of an important instruction found in the version of November 1964: "To teach nothing that might give rise to hatred or contempt for the Jews in the heart of the faithful. . . ." Referring to the defenders of the deicide thesis, of whom Msgr. Carli, Bishop of Segni, made himself the spokesman, and to the pamphleteers who distributed anti-Semitic leaflets at the door from the conciliar aula, Abbé Laurentin is justified in concluding: "The germ of anti-Semitism is therefore not entirely dead, even in the Church, however weakened it may seem." [14]

To be convinced of this, one has only to refer to an Italian work widely circulated at the present time and translated into French: *The Message of the Gospels* by Angelo Alberti.[15] The prefatory letter written by J.-B. Montini, then Archbishop of

[13] *Ibid.*, p. 48.
[14] *Ibid.*, p. 54.
[15] A. Alberti, *The Message of the Gospels* (Paris, 1961), p. 523.

Milan, warmly recommends the book: "Indeed," he writes, "you have written an excellent work and one that is, for many reasons, extremely opportune." Had he read attentively the two central pages (450–51 in the French edition) in which are assembled the finest possible examples of the "education in contempt" with regard to the Jews? Commenting on John 16, 8–11, the author identifies the "world" with the "Jews" without any qualification, and he condemns them all, those of yesterday and those of today, "to wander over the face of the earth". "Destined for perdition" and "accursed by God", "they will be reduced to a mere community of shopkeepers. Such is the punishment of their erroneous judgment." Such an accumulation of nonsense would make one laugh if one did not know too well the fearful consequences of such a teaching.

The revision desired by the Council will be without effect until it achieves the concrete embodiment within the Church of the Council's will to change its outlook and attitude at the deepest level with regard to the Jews. One should also mention—not that it will have much effect—a certain number of customs or medieval traditions still persisting in the Church,[16] the last survivors of Christendom's popular anti-Semitism. There is a revision in process today within the Church. Let us hope that it will bring to a successful conclusion the course of treatment needed to dispel this poison in the Christian conscience and to allow all Christians to look with new eyes on the countenance of Christ's people according to the flesh.

III

THE CHURCH'S INVITATION TO DIALOGUE

By its positive appreciation of the non-Christian religions and their values, whether spiritual, cultural or social, the Declaration *Nostra aetate* is, without any doubt, a gigantic step forward along

[16] P. E. Lapide, *The Last Three Popes and the Jews* (London and New York, 1967).

the path of interfaith dialogue. This is, to our mind, the greatness and the strength of this document. Let us consider, from the point of view that interests us here, the positive and negative sides of this invitation issued by the Church.

1. *The Strength of This Invitation*

Taking as its point of departure the considerable "spiritual patrimony" held in common by Jews and Christians, "the Council desires to encourage and recommend mutual knowledge and esteem; these will arise above all from biblical and theological studies, as well as from fraternal dialogue" (*fraternis colloquiis*).

This could not be better stated. In its request that Christians and Jews come together on the things that unite them—biblical revelation, historical traditions, the messianic hope of the coming kingdom and the spiritual gifts which the God of Jews and Christians has granted them in his grace—the Council is offering an urgent invitation to dialogue among men who have for centuries despised each other. How can one fail to rejoice at this new attitude in the Church which, a few centuries ago, could consider no other form of "dialogue" with the Jews than the effort to convert them with or without their consent? It follows, therefore, that a notable advance has been achieved by Vatican Council II, opening wide the gates of the Church to the non-Christian world in fulfillment of the desire of John XXIII who was a man of dialogue.

But before any dialogue can be begun, certain preliminary conditions must be fulfilled, above all when it is a question of a *Judaeo-Christian* dialogue.[17] Now it does not seem to us that these conditions have been as yet fulfilled by the Church, and that is the weakness of the Council's invitation to dialogue.

2. *The Weakness of This Invitation*

Are the most urgent recommendations and exhortations enough to inaugurate an authentic dialogue between the Church

---

[17] M. De Gadt, *Foi au Christ et dialogues des chrétiens* (Paris, 1967), pp. 134–47.

and Israel? Certainly the dialogue of man with man is always possible. But, at the institutional level, it has one fundamental presupposition—*the recognition of the other in his otherness.*

Up to the present moment there has been no official recognition by the Church of Judaism for what it is and as it defines itself. We have already seen that the Declaration does not speak of "the Jewish religion"—that is, of Judaism as a living contemporary religion with a universal vocation. Until such time as an official declaration has made this recognition, it is meaningless to speak of dialogue between the Church and Judaism. This lacuna in the Declaration is all the more astonishing in that this latter's object was to establish "relations between the Church and the non-Christian religions".

It seems to be the responsibility of the Secretariat for Unity to take up again the "Jewish question" from this angle, since the Jewish question remains within its province.

IV
CONCLUSIONS

To sum up, we are now able to establish the two following signposts on the difficult path of Judaeo-Christian dialogue:

1. The official recognition by the Church of Judaism both as a people and as a contemporary and living religion. The existence of the Jewish people does seem to have been recognized by the Declaration but not, as we have seen, of Judaism as the ethical and religious expression of this people. It follows that Christian theologians, in obedience to the wish of the Council, will be obliged to discover the spiritual riches of *contemporary* Judaism, its social and its cultural values.

2. The extension and concrete application of the Declaration on the Jews. Without this extension and this application, the new "charter of the Christian attitude to the Jews" constituted by the Declaration will remain a dead letter. In the realms of liturgy and catechesis, of theology and history, a revision, an

aggiornamento, begun by Vatican Council II, is indispensable. The abandonment by the Church of a proselytizing attitude to the Jewish people is no less indispensable to the openness and freedom of the Judaeo-Christian dialogue. All these questions are manifestly put to the Church not for the first time, but they are put in a new way, and it would seem that they could well stand a study in depth by Christian exegetes and theologians.

"The Council's vote," in the words of Kevin Fesquet, reporter of *Le Monde,* "turns over a new leaf in the history of the relations between Rome and the Jews." It remains only to write upon this page, as yet unmarked, a new history of the relations between the Church and Judaism, a history compounded of mutual respect, of truth and of friendship.

PART III
DOCUMENTATION
CONCILIUM

Office of the Executive Secretary
Nijmegen, Netherlands

Concilium General Secretariat/*Nijmegen, Netherlands*
Hildegard Goss-Mayr/*Vienna, Austria*

Peace through Revolution

The two encyclicals, *Pacem in terris* of John XXIII and *Populorum progressio* of Paul VI, have met with an uncommon response not only within the Catholic Church but throughout the world. The bearing of both encyclicals had already been tersely summarized in the concept that in our time peace has assumed special importance and has come to mean *development*. Although this development could initially be a factor of unrest, the term nevertheless already prevents peace from being reduced to a sentimental wish or to that passive expectation which follows on war. Absence of war is but a negative aspect of peace.

Peace is also more than is contained in the biblical message of the Churches; it is the result of specialized technical effort. It has become a value in its own right which must be consciously built up and is not yet achieved when the old Christian prayer for deliverance from pest, famine and war has been heard. It demands a coordination of all kinds of efforts in the fields of economics, sociology, psychology, history and humanization, all of which can be gathered under the heading "development". For the West this will mean principally the development of a supranational mentality and an effective extension of research into peace. For what is called the "Third World" it will mainly refer to a new climate of opinions and attitudes which must follow the colonialism of the past and to those technical and economic measures which will make the autonomy of the new nations genuinely viable. For the countries of South America it will mean principally a conscious change in the established order and structures.

These three forms of development will greatly differ in the ways in which they can be worked out. However, they all have in common the underlying thought that an apparently obvious establishment must be replaced by something new. This replacement of the old by the new is clearly not the work of one day. Yet, it is urgently necessary. It is so necessary that, particularly in South America, it is thought that only a revolution can make such a peace possible, and that there is therefore a causal connection between revolution and peace. Peace then becomes the supreme realization of man's rights, to be brought about with as little violence as possible but with violence if necessary.

Sociologists generally agree that all institutions of an established order, the Church included as institutional, are inclined to maintain the established order and in this sense are conservative. The Gospel itself, however, is revolutionary; it pleads for a change of mentality and demands a change in disposition which must constantly nourish the dynamic life of the Church. Since the necessity of a change appears to be urgent in the three sectors of mankind mentioned above for the organization of peace, theology, too, demands that more attention be paid to this dynamic ferment of the Gospel than to the established order of the Church.[1]

[1] Cf. *Concilium* 5 (1965) and 15 (1966), particularly the contributions by R. Coste and F. Böckle. From the abundant literature we refer to some basic studies on the principal aspects of this subject: J. Comblin, *Théologie de la Paix* I (Paris, 1960); II (Paris, 1963); G. Bouthoul, *Traité de sociologie*, ch. III (Paris, 1951); *idem, Avoir la Paix* (Paris, 1961); W. V. O'Brien, *Nuclear War, Deterrence and Morality* (Washington, 1967); W. Schweitzer, *Der entmythologisierte Staat* (Gütersloh, 1968); B. V. A. Roeling, *Over oorlog en vrede* (Amsterdam, 1963); A. Messineo, "L'Organizazione della pace nel mondo contemporaneo," in *Civiltà Catolica* 118 (1967), pp. 358–70; *idem,* "L'Ordine divino della pace e la guerra moderna," *ibid.* (1967), pp. 223–36; *idem, La Violence*

Particularly in South America, about which detailed information will be given in the last part of this article by Hildegard Goss-Mayr, Catholics, too, ask themselves whether the Church should not take an active initiative in this elimination of the established order. There, it is argued, the institutional Church has identified herself with the establishment and thereby slowed down the development of the people. As an institution, she has therefore lost her influence on the real development of society. And so it is there that a most convincing plea is made for a responsible theology of revolution. In this sense, revolution need not yet mean a violent subversion of the establishment, but it may mean an emphasis on precisely those aspects of emancipation which have too long been obstructed by the Church—such aspects as democracy, socialization and the fundamental equality of all men. Now that Marxism offers itself as the best vehicle for this necessary emancipation, the institutional Church is in danger of becoming superfluous in the eyes of many.[2]

Linking this article to the general theme of this volume—namely, the influence of Christian ethics on modern society—we want to limit it to designating those fields where Christian ethics can exercise some influence on two such topical matters as peace and revolution. The title is therefore deliberately paradoxical: "Peace through Revolution", and not something more obvious such as "War and Peace" or "Establishment and Revolution".

(Paris, 1967); *idem, Deutscher Evangelischer Kirchentag Hannover 1967* (Stuttgart/Berlin, 1967). For a survey of the history of the Churches, cf. R. H. Bainton, *Christian Attitudes toward War and Peace* (London, 1961); J. Galtung, *On the Meaning of Non-Violence* (Oslo, 1965); J. C. Bennett, *Foreign Policy in Christian Perspective* (1966); W. Promper, "América Latina," in *Igreja e missao* 16 (1967), pp. 627–35; *idem*, "América Latina em foco," *ibid.*, pp. 799–806; C. Verhoeven, *Tegen het geweld* (Utrecht, 1967); *idem*, "La guerra y la paz," *Criterio* 40 (Dec. 24, 1967), pp. 867–927.

[2] F. van Raalten, "Pazifismus und Ethik," in *Zeitschr. f. Evang. Ethik* 12 (1968), pp. 22–36; J. J. Brieux, "La guérilla en Amérique du Sud," in *Esprit* 35 (Jan. 1968), pp. 35–53; *idem*, "Revolution und Theologie. Das neue in unserm Zeitalter. Ein Symposion," in *Frankfurter Hefte* 22 (Sept. 1967), pp. 616–30.

We shall first deal with the actuality of this subject and then with the present state of theology in these practically virgin fields of peace and revolution. The result will be to show that there is an inner connection between revolution and peace. The concluding section will illustrate the factual possibility of such a non-violent revolution.[3]

I

THE ACTUALITY OF THE SUBJECT

The necessity to start organizing peace as effectively as possible demands that the Churches make their own contribution. The Catholic Church realizes that it is not enough to preach the general message of peace as is done in the two above-mentioned encyclicals. It is not merely a matter for the Church's magisterium; far more is it a matter for lay experts. The authorities have tried to channel the enthusiasm aroused by the two encyclicals and Pope Paul's prophetic address to the United Nations into a more technical organization.

Hence, a special commission has been established, Justitia et Pax (Justice and Peace).[4] This commission is designed for study, not action. It seeks to provide documentation, orientation and practical directives. After the first meeting expectations were high, but after the second this interest yielded to a certain disillusionment because, in the view of one of the most active members, the Brazilian layman Dr. Amoroso Lima, not enough experts were included. And so the commission unintentionally created the impression it wanted to shelve this urgent problem. The unrest that ensued led some 16 bishops from developing countries to address a common message to the faithful of the

[3] R. Rey Alvarez, "L'Amérique latine à la recherche de sa vraie dimension," in *La Rev. Nouv.* 23 (July/August, 1967), pp. 90–101.

[4] "La pace nel magisterio di Paolo VI" and "Difesa e promozione della pace nella dottrina del concilio ecumenico Vaticano II," in *L'Osservatore Romano* (Dec. 31, 1967), pp. 3–4.

Third World in which they pleaded for a concrete application of the principles laid down in *Populorum progressio*.[5]

The Geneva Conference of the World Council of Churches on Church and Society (1966) concentrated on the building up of peace and will bring up the topic again at the 4th General Assembly. This year it will be held during July at Uppsala where it will discuss the possible influence of the Church on what is called "macro ethics", a kind of universal ethics. Although several Churches still hesitate about the inadmissibility of war,[6] the World Council declared that the development of military technology—particularly of atomic, radiological, biological and chemical weapons and the means of using them—marked a decisive turning point in the history of mankind and war. The potential horror of a war which exterminates indiscriminately not only the combatants but also the civilian population, the fact that it will be impossible for the smaller nations to defend themselves, the risk of destroying a whole human culture, the permanent danger for future generations of radioactive matter which is a necessary corollary of the use of nuclear weapons—"all this radically changes the situation of nations and their relations with each other. This new and frightening situation forces Christians to revise what the Churches thought about war and the State's function with regard to war in earlier days. As far back as 1948, the 1st Assembly of the World Council in Amsterdam declared that 'war is against the will of God'. At the same time it recognized three attitudes toward Christian participation in the evil of war, and one was that sometimes war might be the lesser evil. Today the situation is changed. Christians differ as to whether military means may be legitimate in order to achieve aims that are necessary for justice. But atomic warfare exceeds every limit. Mutual nuclear suicide can never establish justice because it

[5] A. Amoroso Lima, "Paix, justice et violence," in *Inf. Cath. Int.* 302 (Dec. 15, 1967); "Right to Revolt. Letter Signed by 17 Bishops," in *The National Catholic Reporter* (Sept. 27, 1967), p. 9.

[6] W. Dirks, "Abschied vom 'gerechten Krieg'," in *Frankfurter Hefte* 22 (July 1967), pp. 489-96.

destroys all that one wants to defend or achieve. We now declare to all governments and all nations that atomic war is against God's will and the greatest of evils. Hence we state that the first duty of governments and their officials is to prevent an atomic war".[6a]

This statement still emphasizes the prevention of wars and it makes the governments principally responsible for it. However, the problem is wider; it concerns the technical buildup of peace and the responsibility of all. A certain number of scientific institutes have been established in recent years throughout the world which, under the heading of polemology (or irenology) or peace research, seek to strip war and peace of the myth of fate and locate them within the scope of scientific human control.[6b] This attempt to place peace within the reach of science has found Catholic support in the international Pax Christi movement which, especially in recent months, has also made direct approaches to various governments. It is convinced that the specifically Christian contribution of the Church to the very complicated problem of peace consists in nourishing the conviction that faith must stimulate the mind to treat the matter scientifically. Faith

[6a] C. P. van Andel, "De dienst van de kerken aan de vrede," in *Rondom het Woord* 10 (Jan. 1968), p. 21.

[6b] Thus, among others, the Canadian Peace Research Institute and the Instituto Espanol de Investigaciones para la paz. Prof. G. Bouthoul founded the Institut de Polémologie of Paris; Prof. J. Galtung is director of the Peace Research Institute of Oslo; Prof. B. Röling directs the Polemologisch Instituut in Groningen and Prof. L. G. A. Schlichting directs the Peace Research Center at the Catholic University of Nijmegen, while Louvain University has its Centre International de Justice sociale. In Sweden there is the Stockholm International Peace Research Institute, and in Japan there is the Hiroshima Institute of Peace Science. In the United States there is among other things the Arms Control and Disarmament Agency, and there are various institutes in Russia, among them the Institute of World Economics and International Relations. Since 1947 there has been a Polish Institute of International Affairs in Poland and there is an Institute of International Politics in Yugoslavia. Cf. J. Galtung, "Peace Research—Science or Politics in Disguise?" in *Intern. Spectator* (Nov. 8, 1967). Details of all institutes may be found in the *International Repertory of Institutions Specializing in Research on Peace* (1966), pp. 29–33, and in *Supplement Intern. Peace Research News Letter* (Nov. 1967), both Unesco publications.

cannot rest content with a utopia of peace. This leads us to the second point of our article: What is new in the problem of peace today?

II

PEACE AS A TECHNICALLY ATTAINABLE HUMAN CONDITION

In spite of the unequivocal rejection of violence by the Gospel, the pagan adage "If you want peace, prepare for war" (*Si vis pacem, para bellum*) has so far prevailed. But this adage is no longer self-evident. Peace cannot be achieved by violence. It can only be built up by "works of peace". The older systems of the period before World War II relied on certain philosophical, theological and juridical ideas to achieve peace. They presupposed that peace depended completely on the free will of man, through evangelical conversion, through education and through better systems of government. Today people are more inclined to use sociology, psychology and the new ideas of history. We are aware of the fact that nationalism, patriotism, national pride, one's own national economic system, one's own culture, etc., are for a large part mythical. Even Thomas Aquinas wondered whether the preservation of one's own territory was sufficient reason to risk a war. But he could also still ask the question whether there was such a thing as a right to war (*jus ad bellum*). The possibility of such a right is denied today because technical development has turned war into such a serious threat to mankind as a whole.

Nevertheless, the great powers try to defend the possession of atomic and nuclear weapons on the basis of the "balance of power". This theory, which is really no longer tenable, rests on the conviction that no nation will contemplate the idea of starting an atomic war on a worldwide scale. The annihilating force of nuclear weapons, the speed with which they can reach their target, the quantity in which they are stored and the nuclear strategy followed by both sides drive home to every potential aggressor that he himself will be destroyed under such circumstances. The function of the weapons has shifted. They are there merely to deter the adversary, not in order to be used, because their use is meaningless. The fact that both sides are aware of this would, on this theory, eliminate world war from history and obstruct minor wars because they would naturally escalate into a world conflict. Peace would then be the fruit of the fear of each other's power.[7]

This theory, supported by a constant effort to keep military force within certain limits, has indeed led to demonstrable results. All the conflicts since World War II have not only been restricted in the kind of weapons used, but also in the range of the conflict and the parties implicated. This modern limitation of the conduct of war has led to a curious change in our thought about war, a change sometimes expressed in the assertion that war is becoming more and more symbolic. But the risk of the unintentional war remains. Nor is it difficult to see that in this theory the element of violence is wholly maintained, even though it is contained in theory.

The Gospel, however, rejects violence itself. Hence there runs side by side with this current, which may be described as "mitigated violence", another current which wants to eliminate violence itself and tries to achieve this for the time being by demanding general disarmament. The first tendency starts from the factual situation while the second will, if necessary, go right against this situation, ready to face the final consequences of non-violent resistance. The first tendency is sometimes described as "realistic" and the second as "prophetic".

Neither the Catholic Church nor any other Christian Church is willing to accept radical pacifism. This may bewilder the prophetic faithful, but one cannot deny that in the "realistic" tendency there is a problem which the Churches cannot abandon by default.[8] Even if general disarmament were achieved and it

---

[7] A. Etzioni, *Winning without War* (New York, 1964).

[8] C. F. von Weiszaecker, *Voorwaarden voor de vrede* (Rotterdam, 1964).

were possible to abolish all atomic weapons, atomic *energy* would remain and its use will expand constantly, if only to solve the problem of energy and keep the world inhabitable. But together with atomic *energy,* atomic *weapons* will always remain within our reach. The difficulty lies in the ambiguity of man. The findings of his science are never pure results but always imply new ethical issues.[9]

For the time being, therefore, the question will remain how man and the structures in which he lives can be adjusted to these new ethical demands. And here, precisely, lies a genuine task for the Churches. B. V. A. Röling, who has done much in Holland to bring about a scientific approach to the problem of peace, refuses to simplify the problem. He points to four fields where science should exercise its influence.

1. Examination of the degree of man's lack of wisdom in his relations with other men; the way in which public opinion is formed; the function of information (the impression of futility, wrongly attributed to the disarmament conference of Geneva, is more the result of systematic disparagement by the mass media than actual fact); the function of the teaching of history; the function of exaggerated national consciousness.

2. Investigation of the conditions which must be fulfilled to make peace possible; this includes the problem of the disparity between rich and poor nations; it also includes a study of whether there is a connection between our need of a new international law and our chances of creating this.

3. Investigation of man's essential historicity and, in this connection, investigation of war, the way conflicts arise from man's aggressiveness and the still limited realization of his social structures.

4. Investigation of the measures that may lead to another way of thinking and of the role which can be played here by the Churches, the artists, the mass-media and public discussion.

[9] G. Hower, "Die atomäre Bewaffnung als geistesgeschichtliches und theologisches Problem," in *Atomzeitalter, Krieg und Frieden* (Berlin, 1962).

In brief, we must have a systematic investigation of the causes and functions of war (polemology), the conditions required to achieve peace (irenology) and the means of translating this factually established need into reality by cooperation of the governments. It is not a neutral science, detached from human values, but a practical science which constantly seeks to penetrate politics. Reflection and scientific investigation are necessary in order to take peace out of the realm of utopia and to turn it into something that in principle is attainable as a form of humanization.[10]

A first phase in this labor of long duration will be the unmasking of evidence, in any form, as an appropriate means of achieving this stage of humanization and the creation of a less utopian image of peace. Peace is a sober technical job, more the unimpressive result of communication and unity than an overemphasized ethical effort. If we direct our vigilance only to the final result, peace, we are already launched into a dialogue with violence and preparing for war. The objection that we shall never succeed without violence has already been disproved by Gandhi's non-violent method at the time of India's independence. It is obviously naive to maintain that we can create an effective peace in the world with the Sermon on the Mount, but Christian morality might well emphasize more outspokenly the non-violence which is the basic directive contained in that sermon.

Although this subject was extensively discussed at Vatican Council II,[11] there was no desire to deal with practical measures (such as the right of conscientious objection); on the other hand, peace was linked with the expectation of salvation and more concretely with the demands of social justice. The hope of peace, expressed by the Council, is based on the theology of the ultimate reconciliation of all men. The Council pointed out that human conflicts are rooted in human deficiency and sinfulness. The building of peace cannot overlook the redemption. The danger is

[10] T. F. Lentz, *Toward a Science of Peace* (New York, 1955), p. 3.
[11] P. Ramsey, "The Vatican Council on Modern War," in *Theological Studies* 27 (1966), pp. 179–203; J. B. Hirschmann, "Dienst am Frieden," in *Stimmen der Zeit* 91 (1966), pp. 113–22.

that this redemption may be presented as something external. The ethic of the Christian redemption, however, implies that we must first do the possible in order to achieve the as yet impossible. If the Church wants to continue to preach redemption, this must imply a technical effort to bring peace within the scope of human achievement. On the other hand, belief in redemption is indispensable if we do not want to be discouraged in our efforts for peace.

III

REVOLUTION

When what we traditionally call "peace" is threatened by the fact that power is concentrated in the hands of the few and in danger of leading to violence, can we still use the idea of revolution in connection with peace? Revolution always implies a certain margin of violence.[12] On the other hand, if peace is related to development, it must be admitted that, particularly in South America and in the Third World, the situation is such that the established order is a permanent obstacle to development and can apparently only be overcome by means of a revolution. As a result, there is keen interest in those countries in revolution, even among theologians.

The previously mentioned message of the sixteen bishops to the underdeveloped nations shows an attitude which wants to go beyond *Populorum progressio:* "After the Council, powerful voices were raised to demand a stop to this close association of the Church with capitalism . . . of which the Church is accused in various quarters. . . . We ourselves have the duty to examine our situation seriously on this point and to free our Churches from every servility with regard to large financial concerns. . . . Whenever a system ensures the well-being of a few at the expense of the common good, the Church not only

---

[12] P. Régamey, "The Mystique of Non-Violent Action," in *The Thought* 41 (1966), pp. 381–90.

must expose this injustice, but detach herself from such an iniquitous system, ready to cooperate with another system that is better adjusted to the needs of our age and more just. . . . Christians are obliged to prove that Christianity is the true socialism if it is fully lived in the just distribution of wealth and basic equality. . . . The first task of the deprived nations and the poor of those nations is to bring about their own development." [13]

In the context which distinguishes between good and bad revolutions, necessary and superfluous revolutions, non-violent and violent revolutions, it is obvious that, on reading this message from the bishops, one thinks of revolution. But this can be non-violent in the form of a social and economic revolution. Perhaps the word "revolution" is too heavily tainted with the violence of the Marxist revolution for Christians to become easily enthusiastic about this message. When Bishop Podestà of Avellanada, a working-class suburb of Buenos Aires, was forced to resign by the government because he courageously promoted this line of thought in *Populorum progressio,*[13a] some concluded that the official course of the Church is still different from that indicated in the bishops' message. Nor can one be surprised that people thought here of a violent revolution. The use of violence is increasing in the world. In the beginning of 1958 there were 23 rebellions of some duration in the world. On February 1, 1966 there were 40. The total number of violent revolutions on a minor scale has grown every year. There were 34 in 1958, 58 in 1965.

The most important factor in this context is that there is a direct and demonstrable connection between this violence and the economic situation of the suffering nations. The 27 richest countries possess 75% of the wealth of the world, although they have only 25% of the world's population. Since 1958 only one of these 27 countries had an important internal rising within its own territory. Of the 38 very poor countries—with a per capita in-

---

[13] Cf. *The National Catholic Reporter* (Sept. 27, 1967), p. 9.

[13a] "Substanzwandel des Oekumenischen—Testfall: Lateinamerika," in *Herder-Korrespondenz* 20 (1966), p. 484; *Inf. Cath. Intern.* 302 (Dec. 15, 1967), p. 11; J. Mejía, "El retiro del obispo de Avellanada," in *Criterio* 40 (Dec. 24, 1967), pp. 930–31.

come of 90 dollars per year—32 suffered from serious conflicts, averaging two outbursts of violence per year during a period of eight years. In countries with less poverty there is also less conflict.[14]

Safety is not the same as the possession of arms; today safety is secured through development. But development is not "alms on a large scale", nor the exporting of a prosperous culture to underdeveloped countries, but primarily the recognition of these countries' basic right to partnership and the development of ecomic structures at world level, combined with the development of a strong supranational structure. Development is not based on an appeal to generosity but on social justice, realizing that a certain degree of development (300 dollars per person per year) creates material for conflict. There seems to be only one way of countering this violence—to promote development effectively. Fr. Lebret, who took a large part in the composition of *Populorum progressio,* had written before the encyclical appeared: "Latin America needs a radical change in the mentality of its leading classes. If these cannot cooperate with the people on the basis of constructive planning and so bring about a peaceful revolution, a bloody revolution is inevitable."

The refusal or acceptance of violence in bringing about a revolution is the point which divides the thinking people in South America. That there must be revolution is agreed, and it has already been present since 1964 both in the violent way of guerilla warfare and the non-violent way of a change in mentality.

The division here is not, strange to say, between Marxists and Christians; not all Marxists are for violence, and not all Christians for non-violence. Both ways have their protagonists among Marxists and Christians. Supporters of the violent method are Fidel Castro, Che Guevara and the priest, Camilo Torres (edu-

---

[14] *Eglise et société—Une enquête oecuménique* (Geneva, 1966); G. Drekonja, "Das Experiment des Eduardo Frei. Die ideologische Gärung in Lateinamerika," in *Wort und Wahrheit* 22 (Nov. 1967), pp. 679–712; P. Bouin, "Les forces révolutionnaires en Amérique Latine," in *Terre entière* 23 (May–June 1967), pp. 31–106; *Christian Students and the Asian Revolution* (Colombo, 1967).

cated at Louvain University), while the Frenchman Régis De-
bray propounds the theory of the "revolution within the revolution", for which he refers to the successful revolution in Cuba.
A. B. Fragoso, Bishop of Crateus in northern Brazil, sees in
Cuba more evangelical inspiration than people are inclined to
credit it with. This violent revolution is systematically boycotted
by such conservative elements as the Inter-American Peace Force
of the U.S.A. The non-violent way is effectively inspired by
some prominent members of the South American hierarchy,
such as Helder Camara of Recife, Mendez Arceo of Cuernavaca,
R. Larrain of Talca (who died tragically in 1967), J. McGrath,
one of the pioneers of Schema XIII and Msgr. Guzman, professor at the University of Bogotà and a friend of Torres.

The non-violent revolution seeks to achieve at a world level
what the socialist movement has already achieved in the Western
world and to eliminate the proletariat by integrating it into the
whole production process of the world in a way worthy of man.
But this cannot be done without changing the economic system
of Western Europe and the United States. In this context the
name "Third World" makes one think of the *tiers état* of the
French Revolution. Genuine aid toward development must break
into the structures of the Third World, but this requires a great
deal of sacrifice on the part of affluent Western capitalism. Along
these lines there is a connection with scientific peace research
in the United States and Western Europe, which sees in the
industrialization of the developing countries one of the main
factors in the building up of peace.

The scope of this task becomes clear when we remember that
the share of the developing countries in the total industrial production of the world is only 5%. An analysis of UNIDO (the
latest U.N. organization for industrial development) shows that
if things remain as they are at the moment, the industrial share
of the developing countries will still be only 6 or 7% by 1990.
And here lies a major task for the Churches and their mission.
No wonder that the theology of the mission will have to include

more and more development aid in its reflection on what the real meaning is of the mission in this age.[15]

We conclude this article with a report on the success of a non-violent revolution on a small scale as detailed by Hildegard Goss-Mayr who was actively involved in its progress.

IV

A NON-VIOLENT REVOLUTION

I know the misery and the hope of Latin America. I know the great changes shaking this subcontinent, which is engaged in making the leap from a feudalistic and early capitalist form of society—the legacy of its colonial past—into the second half of the 20th century, an age which demands human dignity and human rights for every citizen.

The reasons for the subcontinent's misery are numerous and complex. Here we can mention only a few of them: the *large estates,* for example, with their archaic, unprofitable methods of husbandry (1½% of the landowners of Latin America own 50% of the fertile land, only a fraction of which is cultivated). The owners of these estates obstinately oppose any kind of agrarian reform which aims to raise production by means of rational, planned management and to secure justice and human dignity for the farm laborers by altering the conditions of ownership. In extensive areas of Latin America *laborers* and *tenant farmers* still live today like slaves, in complete dependence on the landowners, in hunger, misery and ignorance. (Half the population of Latin America is illiterate; in depressed areas such as the northeast of Brazil child-mortality is about 50%. In spite of this high rate of child-mortality the population is still increasing by 2½%–3% every year.)

I have seen the despair of mothers holding dead children in

[15] The Documentation section of the next volume of *Concilium* will be devoted to this question.

their arms and not knowing how they were to feed the living ones. The bravest of these people make up their minds to *emigrate* to the towns. Hundreds of thousands, even millions of Latin Americans have moved into the towns or are on their way there in the search for work, bread, housing and educational possibilities for their children. They surround the towns with continually growing slums. In many cases the inhabitants of the slums already form half the population of the big cities. *Unemployment,* rootlessness and lack of schools and vocational training make the slums of Bogotà and Lima, of Santiago and Buenos Aires, of São Paulo, Rio and Recife—to mention only a few—some of the grimmest sights on earth.

Provoked by the affluence of the middle and upper classes and denied any possibility of bettering themselves, these people form perfect breeding-grounds for future rebellions. Even those who have the luck to find jobs in industry are frequently confronted in their work with manifestations of *classical capitalism,* which sees in the worker only a means to the attainment of the largest possible profit and treads his rights underfoot (in numerous Latin American countries the trade unions are controlled by the industrialists and are therefore ineffective). In Recife I knew a worker with seven children—I mention this only to bring home the situation to the reader—who became insane when he lost his job.

But the misery of Latin America is also caused by factors which lie outside the Third World and in the highly industrialized countries. People are beginning to recognize these factors today. Here are just a few examples: the continually *falling prices paid for raw materials* by the industrial countries to the developing countries (so far raw materials are the chief export of the Third World); the *debts incurred by the developing countries* and their consequent *economic and political dependence* on the industrial states (in this connection it is worth pointing to the dangerous effects of bilateral economic agreements); the *drawing of large profits* from concerns set up in Latin America by the businessmen of highly industrialized countries, etc. It is clear even from these few indications that the economy of Latin America and other developing regions can only be put on a sound basis, and truly human conditions of life can only be created for the inhabitants of these regions, if our mentality and our economic policy undergo a radical change.

Growing Awareness

The situation described above is not new. The fresh and decisive factor today is the fact that the population of the areas concerned is growing more and more aware of its misery, is beginning to rebel against it, and is starting to seek ways of freeing itself from this misery. Thus in many parts of the subcontinent a revolutionary situation is arising and steadily growing more tense. The historical process—in which we recognize humanity's path to fulfillment in God—demands that new and continually wider sections of humanity should achieve responsibility in society. Once it was the middle class, then the working class, of Europe; now it is the underprivileged masses in the developing countries, especially in Latin America, who are struggling for equality, for the right to share the goods of the earth and also to make their contribution to the upward climb of humanity. How long will it be before their patience is exhausted?

In the long run no power in the world can prevent the necessary revolutionary changes. This urge for equality and social justice is the outward sign of God's activity in history. The people in Latin America who have recognized the situation not only possess the moral right to fight for revolutionary changes; they are in fact obliged as responsible human beings to do all in their power to improve the lives and secure the rights of their fellow creatures.

Is it necessary to ask *where a Christian must stand in this situation? Pacem in terris,* Vatican Council II, the Congress on "Church and Society" held by the World Council of Churches at Geneva in the summer of 1966 and *Populorum progressio* have made it quite clear that the Church must stand on the side of the disfranchised and oppressed. Still clearer is the statement, published jointly by 17 bishops of the Third World in the summer of 1967, which says: "The Church knows that the Gospel demands the first and radical revolution, which is known as conversion." This conversion has "a relation to the community which is of grave importance to society as a whole. . . . Poor people and poor countries, among whom the merciful Lord has placed us as shepherds of a small flock, know from experience that they must rely more on themselves and on their own strength than on the help of the rich. . . .": *Témoignage Chrétien* VIII (Paris, 1967), p. 31.

What Does the Reality Look Like?

The Churches of Latin America, both the evangelical Churches and the Catholic Church, are deeply committed *to the traditional camp* which believes that in the existing circumstances it must protect democracy and freedom, which suspects Communist machinations behind any attempt at reform, however moderate, and which wards off a new order with all the means at its disposal (money, political influence, military and economic power, etc.). Even today large sections of the hierarchy, clergy and laity still belong to these circles; indeed it is not long since the Churches—not only in Latin America—supported almost without exception the forces that represented at any given time the status quo.

On the other hand, in Latin America there is a *steadily growing Christian minority,* numbering among its members bishops, priests and laymen, which has recognized the injustice prevailing and has taken up its position decidedly and radically on the side of the poor. Together with the poor they are seeking and treading new paths. Their aim is not only to alleviate misery by charitable means but also to create a society in which everyone can lead a dignified human life. These groups are being joined by more and more members of the younger generation—students, intellectuals, social workers, workmen, trade union leaders and priests—and many poor people put their hope in them.

But now comes the decisive question: *In what way can the*

hopes of the poor be fulfilled? Does Christianity, on the basis of *the Gospel, have a special contribution to make to the revolution* *and, if so, what is it?* A great deal is said and written today about revolution, but my experiences in Latin America have confirmed my opinion that theology and the Church have not yet uttered the final and most essential word on this subject; moreover, I feel that the truly Christian contribution to the necessary changes is neither being preached nor—apart from a few exceptions—being put into effect. Once again—and more clearly than ever before—our Church is confronted with the demand to make the revolutionary power of the Gospel effective in a situation in which, without the Christian contribution, a solution can only be achieved by the traditional path of violence and war (one has only to think of the modern methods of warfare being used in Vietnam as the conflict escalates further and further).

In these circumstances I would like to make an urgent appeal to Christian theologians to explain clearly and unambiguously the contribution which the Gospel of justice and love has to make to the revolutionary changes emerging in Latin America. This would enable the laity to apply effectively, in the struggle for justice, the genuine, humane alternative that corresponds to the dignity of man. Much more than signs is demanded of the Church; she is expected to collaborate energetically in fulfilling peoples' hopes.

Who in Latin America today is offering those who have recognized the need for change any concrete ways, means and methods of putting the revolution into effect? Almost all efforts are based on the Marxist theory of revolution developed in the 19th century and applied in our own, even though different variations on it are being thought out and prepared for use. On one essential point all the revolutionary groups are unanimous: all means, including civil war, guerilla warfare, murder, extortion and hatred, are not only permissible but necessary in order to attain the goal of revolutionary change through the erection of a new structure of society. "Hatred [is] a factor in the struggle," wrote Che Guevara, "unyielding hatred of the enemy, a hatred that drives man beyond the natural limits and converts him into an effective, vigorous, selective and cold machine for killing. Our soldiers must be like this; a people without hatred cannot defeat a brutal enemy" (Che Guevara, *Letter to the Executive Secretariat of OSPAAL,* Berlin, 1967).

Let us have no illusions about this. A glance at Vietnam is sufficient to bring home to us what it means to be members of the Vietcong, guerilla fighters or part of the civil population in a country in the grip of revolution. These theories about revolution are rational; they aim at achieving the greatest effectiveness, they strive for justice and they are developed without exception by idealistic men who are concerned to gain political power, on the basis of which a new order of society is to be built up. But these theories are conceived by people to whom *the Gospel and its message* is alien; they are building on *pre-Christian conceptions.*

This Marxist theory of revolution is today the only one available to Christians of South America who seek genuine involvement. If many, and not infrequently the best, young Christians choose this path, *it is because they know no other,* because theology and the Church offer them in their crisis of conscience nothing but the *just war*—under whatever name it may be fought (war of liberation, defensive war, etc.). The antithesis between the Gospel of love and the revolution of violence and hatred is a tragic conflict in which these young men are offered no alternative by the Church.

Among European Catholics too, one hears a good deal about Camilo Torres and the revolutionary Christians. Are not people even in Christian circles in Europe only too ready to justify, in a theology of revolution, means which are in radical contradiction with the message of Christ? Realizing that they have identified themselves far too long with the status quo, people make the leap into the revolutionary camp without being clearly aware what hard, indeed insoluble, conflicts of conscience a man like Camilo Torres and hundreds of thousands of his fellow countrymen have to endure before making their decision. Has the Gospel of love and justice nothing to offer, then, in this struggle for justice? I met Camilo Torres in 1962, a few days after arriving in Latin America for the first time. We talked for nearly a whole night about the contribution of the Gospel to the revolution. Toward the end of the conversation, Camilo Torres told us how deeply conscious he was that under his hands, the hands of a priest, the perfect sacrifice of divine love was consummated, and that it formed the pattern for the transformation of the world. Previously, he said, he had made this love effective only in a limited way, in relation to the poor; the rich he had written off. But the revolution of the Gospel must build on the Lord's total love and fight the battle with the weapons he has shown to us. Yet during his theological studies no one had taught him to fight with these weapons, and in Colombia there was no practical experience in their use. He said: "Come back and work with us; together we shall perhaps make it the path to life and hope for our people." But as new arrivals, with no experience of the situation, we were unable to accept his suggestion at that time. Yet should we have done so? Camilo Torres, a man of faith with a talent for leadership, pursued logically the path of the *bellum justum,* the path which he had been taught and knew, to his death as a guerilla fighter. Theology and the Church did not help him to testify to that particular revolutionary power which is an essential part of the evangelical message.

Where Does the Gospel's Contribution to the Revolution Lie?

What do the bishops of the Third World mean when they say in their statement: "The Church knows that the Gospel demands the first and radical revolution . . . which [has] a relation to the community and which is of grave importance to society as a whole." What does Chapter 5 of the *Pastoral Constitution on the Church in the Modern World* mean when it speaks of those means of defense "which are also at the disposal of the weak"? I should like to indicate here briefly what I, together with nu-

merous other Christians in Europe and Latin America, understand the Christian faith to mean when it refers to the revolutionary power of the Gospel. Developing, proclaiming and applying seem to us to be the Church's most pressing tasks in this
revolutionary situation. May our theologians and our Church
enlarge this testimony into a constructive, creative alternative
in the struggle for justice!

Is it not a question of uncovering and making effective that
power and strength in man which God the Father revealed to
us when he replied to the revolt, the hatred, the injustice and all
the sins of mankind not with fresh hatred, violence and destruction but by overcoming the evil of all ages through the highest
act of divine love, the sacrifice of his Son? Did not God wish to
reveal to us by this act that evil and injustice can only be overcome in the last resort by the power of justice and love—love
of one's enemy, divine love—and not by the evil means employed
by human beings for thousands of years? He revealed this divine
power to us through Christ's teaching, through his life and
through his death on the cross. During the third year of his
public ministry Jesus indicated the injustice that has been done
and still exists; he condemned it and confronted man's conscience with the truth. Through Christ this power of truth and
justice is established in every man and can become effective in
every man.

Moreover, the act of redemption gives expression to God's
unshakable trust in man: God builds on man's conscience, on
his capacity to change himself. The Christian is called to model
himself on Christ and to fight with the power of love and justice
to conquer injustice in himself and around him—that is, in society—in order to help build up an order of society that treats
man with respect. The object is not to destroy the opponent,
but, by the conduct of the disfranchised and the power of this
justice and love, to make such an urgent onslaught on the conscience of those responsible; in this way, such strong pressure
will be exerted on those in power that the machinery which legal-
izes injustice will be forced to come to a halt and to function

according to new laws. The old concept of an eye for an eye, a tooth for a tooth, has been superseded by a new, creative attitude and by the onslaught of the power of divine justice and love on the conscience of all those, both individuals and groups, responsible for injustice. In this way evil is tackled at the root and overcome, and the situation is transformed. Never did Christ pass over injustice in silence, and never must the Christian pass over injustice in silence; he must fight it with the new weapons provided by Christ for the conquest of injustice. As for the opponent responsible for the injustice, there is the possibility of conversion and collaboration in the common good.

To the poor, who today are left to anyone who will provide them with weapons to obtain power for themselves—for they are poor in education, influence, money and weapons—*the Gospel, as the message of hope, offers the whole power of divine justice and love,* forces which reside in the poor themselves and only need to be awakened and put to practical use. The struggle with the weapons of non-violence (the expression can be allowed to stand in the absence of a better one) or, perhaps better, the struggle based on the power of justice and love, leads the poor man to self-reliance and development and makes him collaborate in the formation of the new society. Since this struggle, in contrast to armed revolution, is not dependent on the support of a financial, military or political kind from one of the big power blocs, and since its "poor" weapons testify to the justice of its cause, it runs far less danger of being involved in ideological clashes between the great powers and offers the chance of genuine, democratic development.

In order to be effective in the context of a developing region like Latin America, the non-violent revolution must be prepared and carried out on several levels simultaneously. *The non-violent struggle begins at the bottom* with the education of the consciences of farm and industrial workers and their training for the fight (cf. the methods of Gandhi and Martin Luther King). It leads from dialogue to direct action, to strikes, civil disobedience, immobilization and an increasingly powerful moral and physical pressure on the persons and institutions embodying injustice.

The efforts at the grass roots must be coordinated and directed at the *national level*. At this level the new legal foundations must be created by negotiations secured by means of this activity at the bottom. (The collaboration and assistance of experts is indispensable.) But it is inconceivable that non-violent action in a Latin American country should become an effective force unless at least a section of the Church stands behind it; unless theologians work out and teach this doctrine of the revolutionary power of the Gospel, and unless bishops and priests support the planning and preparation, allow the churches to be used as centers of action, and portray this struggle as the logical outcome of Christian faith and life, it cannot be successful.

However, non-violent action in developing regions can only become a reality if it is embarked upon with *the same resolution in Europe and the U.S.A.*—that is, if the industrialized countries adopt those radical changes in their attitude and economic conceptions which are a pre-condition for the economic and social recovery of the Third World. This demands perceptible sacrifices, a genuine appreciation of the need for worldwide solidarity and the knowledge that our highly industrialized world is also dependent for its stability on a harmonious understanding between rich and poor. These changes can only be made possible by the planned cooperation of the special agencies of the United Nations with economic experts, trade unions, businessmen, politicians, etc., and by steady educational work on the part of the Churches. It will take nothing less than a hard and tireless struggle of this sort to alter the egotistic attitudes deeply embedded in every layer of our welfare society and to bring about the revolution demanded by the whole world.

In the summer of 1967, we ran training courses on non-violence in various Latin American countries, courses which were attended by, among others, representatives of movements which can no longer see any way forward except through violent revolution. At that time we noted repeatedly that as non-violent action became a reality and a visible sign of genuine transformation, many people who had opted in principle for violent resistance were ready to cooperate, since what they were interested in was not the armed struggle itself, but man and the restoration of justice. The call for non-violent action was particularly convincing wherever concrete examples at the grass roots could be described, as, for example, in Brazil.

Finally, the essential thing is to present the non-violent revolution as a more humane, more appropriate and more creative way—since it is the one revealed by God—of overcoming injustice and renewing the basic structure of society.

To give the reader a better understanding of what has been said above, I will conclude with a short account of a "grassroots" action carried out in Brazil during the strike at Perus.

The Strike at Perus

Perus is a suburb of São Paulo containing a large cement works. Since 1954 Dr. Mario Carvalho de Jesus, an outstanding Christian lawyer, has looked after a trade union in this factory. The trade unions of Brazil are as numerous as they are ineffective. They are frequently under the influence of the factory owners and therefore cannot carry out their real task, that of representing the rights of the workers. Mario de Jesus, the father of eight children, has not only put his knowledge, his private means and his energies at the service of the workers; in the last analysis it is his faith that gives him the strength to weather even the most difficult situations and to promote efforts for social justice. Under his leadership the strike at Perus became the most important demonstration of non-violent revolution achieved in Brazil up to this time.

The immediate cause of the strike at Perus, which began in 1962, was the fact that the workers' pay was *four months* in arrears and agreements to build houses for them, a project for which the firm retained a portion of their pay, were not being kept. The proprietor of the cement works at Perus is one of the most powerful and influential men in the country, but he is well known for his anti-social working conditions. He combines economic power with financial power and political influence. Prior to 1965, he was a member of the Brazilian parliament.

In the face of this powerful management, the workers felt weak and helpless; they had to bow to the situation so as not to lose their jobs. But in 1962 there was a fresh development. The trade union group centered around Mario de Jesus made the decision to tackle the situation. The injustice was no longer tolerable. As a Christian, one cannot accept injustice in silence, especially when the injustice is being done to one's fellowmen. About 800 workers went on strike for fair wages and observance of the agreement about housing.

None of the workers, and not even Mario de Jesus, could foresee in 1962 that this strike would last five years and constitute the beginning of a long struggle for the workers' basic rights. It was the start not simply of a battle over the problem of Perus but of a battle destined to show the whole country that it was possible with the weapon of the poor, the weapon of non-violence, to assert oneself against mighty capitalistic enterprises and to obtain justice.

Immediately after the beginning of the strike the factory owner began to employ every kind of slander and pressure. He sought to shatter the unity of the union, discriminated against the striking workers, and even tried bribery as the case went up to higher and higher courts. His purpose in all this was to make the strikers capitulate. It seems a miracle that the group stood fast. This "miracle" lay mainly in Mario de Jesus' tremendous faith, which communicated itself to the workers and their families.

I remember a meeting of the Perus strikers in 1964. They had gathered with their wives and families in a wooden shed. (A strike involving the worker's livelihood, when he turns against an injustice that threatens the family at its root, concerns everyone—men, women and children). When Dr. Mario spoke to these tired, waiting people, he used scarcely any other words than those of the Gospel: "Christ has given to us men," he said, "the invincible power of divine love, which is the weapon and power of the poor; by our fight for justice and for the lives of our families and comrades, unjustice is being gradually overcome; we are all responsible for seeing that injustice is overcome in the consciences and hearts of the powerful and influential; our struggle is helping to free the worker of Brazil from his inhuman situation and to give him an example how to fight and become responsible. This great aim is certainly worth the sacrifice which we are making ourselves!" At these words one man after another gained new courage and looked with more hope and confidence at the hard days and months that lay before them. They went quietly back home, determined to carry on the fight.

It need hardly be said that there were crises to overcome and difficult problems to solve. At first there was no money with which to pay the strikers. In a developing country in which unemployment prevails and inadequate wages are paid, solidarity is weak. Everyone concentrates on the struggle for his own survival. Yet in numerous factories it was possible to evoke a feeling of solidarity which made it possible to continue the strike.

There was also the temptation to use force. The grinding negotiations, which did not seem to lead to any result, exhausted the patience of many workers. They doubted the possibility of ever reaching a solution without the application of force. They toyed with the idea of killing the factory owner. "And what," asked Dr. Mario, "shall we solve by that? We shall give those in power an excuse to arrest us and to nullify our efforts. We shall have neither changed the industrialists nor achieved anything for the Brazilian worker. The situation would be worse than before. No, our strength lies in respect for man, whether it be our employer, the chief of police or one of us. Our strength lies in helping right to triumph by means of our moral pressure."

How deep the industrialists' hatred was for those who were attacking their concept of life and their privileges will be illustrated by the following incident. On the road to Perus, which runs in places through areas that are not yet built up, Dr. Mario was threatened one day by the proprietor of Perus with a pistol. With the firm conviction that if necessary he must be prepared to sacrifice himself for his comrades, Dr. Mario answered quietly: "Carry on and shoot if you think that in this way you can do away with the problem. But justice will triumph even without me." The factory owner did not shoot the defenseless man down; had he sensed in him a strength against which his weapon was powerless?

During the five years of the strike, Dr. Mario, with the help of the workers of Perus, also performed another equally important work without which no really thorough revolution is possible: by means of a continual, untiring *dialogue* he influenced every sector of public opinion that was concerned with the problem of the workers, and step by step he won sympathy and even cooperation. When the strike began, the press, ecclesiastical circles (except for a very few bishops), politicians and judges were all prejudiced against Mario and the workers since the strike signified a direct attack on tradition, privilege and the status quo. Through innumerable conversations, contacts and expressions of opinion, as well as through the workers' attitude which excluded hatred, it was gradually realized that here human rights, justice and sheer Christianity were involved. In the spring of 1967 37 bishops adopted a position favoring the strikers of Perus. The attitude of the press became more positive and a change in that of the law was also perceptible. The case went up from the local labor tribunal in São Paulo to the Supreme Court in Rio de Janeiro. The first three hearings were decided in favor of the management. Dr. Mario had nothing to put forward but the true facts, which he also explained personally to all the lawyers engaged in the case.

Slowly a change became perceptible. At the fourth hearing the Supreme Court sent the case back to a lower court and ordered a fresh hearing there. This took place in the spring of 1967 and was decided in favor of the workers. This decision not only meant that for the first time in Brazil social justice had been secured by means of a strike, but it also implied that the strike as such is a legitimate weapon of the workers in their fight for their rights. In addition, this thoroughgoing demonstration of non-violent action showed a new way of fighting for the defeat of injustice even against powerful economic groups.

In May 1967, the strike reached a final climax which proved as never before that non-violence is really the weapon of the poor. The occasion was a three-week strike at Perus over a question of social rights. The strikers were keeping watch day and night in front of the factory to prevent the strike from being broken by non-union labor. There were repeated disputes with the police who wanted to provoke the strikers to acts of violence in order to have an excuse to arrest them. But the workers would not be provoked. They resisted in a quiet and disciplined way, determined to carry on the strike until they obtained their rights.

However, one morning the factory owner made up his mind to persuade other workers, by paying them excessively high wages, to carry on in place of the strikers. Among the thousands of unemployed there were many who were ready to betray their comrades and accept the offer. (Hunger and need destroy solidarity.) Finally it came to the point where sacks of cement were being loaded on to lorries and preparations were being made to drive them away. The gate in front of which the strikers were keeping watch opened and the first lorry drove out.

It was a dramatic moment. Were the strikers to admit defeat through the treachery of their comrades, give up the strike and let injustice take its course? They could not do this; they dared not do this.

First one, then two and finally several stretched out on the ground in front of the approaching lorries; they felt it better to die, to give up their lives in the effort to obtain justice and decent conditions for themselves and their comrades rather than yield to cowardly bribery. They were fathers of families. They risked their lives for thousands of families whose children deserved to grow up as free and respected human beings.

The lorry drove up. The driver did not hesitate; he had been paid. He would drive over the men lying on the ground. Was it not their own fault? Only a short stretch to go and the deed would be done. But at this moment a policeman rushed up, then a second, then several. They stationed themselves determinedly between the lorry and the men stretched out on the ground waiting for death. No longer, they felt, could they protect the factory owner's interests; no longer could they carry out this order. It could not be right; it was inhuman. Their consciences were touched by the courage and heroism of these workers, who were ready to die for the sake of justice. Right was on their side; of that there could be no doubt.

Trembling and covered in sweat, the men rose from the red dust of the road. The strike was successful. Justice had triumphed; it had overcome bribery and the power of the police. From that day on, the workers of Peru knew more clearly than ever before that non-violence is the weapon of the poor. The strike was victorious. There was hope for their own lives and for those of the generations to come.

BIOGRAPHICAL NOTES

WILHELM KORFF: Born in Germany in 1926, he was ordained in 1952. He studied at the Major Seminary of Cologne and at the University of Bonn, receiving his doctorate in theology in 1965. His thesis was published in Cologne in 1966 under the title *Ehre, Prestige, Gewissen.*

ROGER GARAUDY: Born in France in 1913, he is a Marxist atheist. He holds a degree in philosophy, is a doctor of letters, and teaches at the Faculty of Letters in Poitiers. He is Director of the Marxist Study Center in Paris. Among his published works are *Qu'est-ce que la morale marxiste?* (Paris, 1963), *Marxisme du XXème Siècle* (Paris, 1966) and *From Anathema to Dialogue* (London, 1967).

CHRISTOPH WAGNER: Born in Germany in 1929, he is a Catholic. He studied at the Free University of Berlin, at Oberlin and Colorado Colleges in the United States, and at the Universities of Heidelberg and Wurzburg. He received his doctorate in philosophy, and has been a business consultant since 1964. He is the author of "Arbeitsteilung und Kirche," in *Pastoralblatt* 12 (Cologne, 1967).

ALDO FERRER: Born in Buenos Aires in 1927, he studied at the Faculty of Economic Science of the National University of Buenos Aires and received his doctorate in that subject. He is professor of political economy for the Argentine at the National University of La Plata, and has been assessor of the Pan-American Development Bank since 1961. Since 1956 he has been a member of the Argentine delegation to the Economic Council of the United Nations. His publications include *La Economía Argentina—Las etapas de su desarrollo y problemas actuales* (Mexico).

PHILIPP HERDER-DORNEICH: Born in Germany in 1928, he is a Catholic. He holds a degree in the science of economics, receiving his doctorate in political science in 1957. He is dean of studies at the University of Cologne and honorary professor at the University of Innsbruck. He is also director of the Forschungsinstitut für Einkommenspolitik und Soziale Sicherung in Cologne. His published works include *Zur Theorie der sozialen Steuerung* (Cologne, 1965) and *Sozialökonomische Theorie der Gesetzlichen Krankenversicherung* (Cologne, 1966).

JANKO MUSULIN: Born in Austria in 1916, he is a Catholic. A writer and journalist, with a degree in engineering, he works with the Viennese publishers Fritz Molden Verlag. From 1958 to 1962 he was editor-in-chief of *Neue Rundschau.*

GÜNTER STRUCK: Born in Germany in 1923, he studied at the University of Bonn where he received his doctorate in medicine. From 1952 to 1964 he was an assistant in the University Clinics of Cologne, Bonn and Freising, and is now director of the Kath. Zentralinstitut für Ehe- und Familienfragen in Cologne. His publications include *Ehenot-Ehehilfe* (Lahn-Verlag, 1966), and he has written many articles on neurology, psychology and pathology.

FRANZ FURGER: Born in Switzerland in 1935, he was ordained in 1961. He studied at Louvain and at the Gregorian in Rome, receiving doctorates in philosophy and moral theology. Since 1965 he has taught philosophy at the Faculty of Theology in Lucerne. His publications include *Struktureinheit der Wahrheit bei Jaspers* (Salzburg, 1960) and *Gewissenund Klugheit* (Lucerne, 1965).

JEAN-PAUL LICHTENBERG, O.P.: Born in France in 1930, he was ordained in 1967. He studied at the Faculties of Philosophy and Theology at the Saulchoir. He is chaplain and an active member of the Peace Movement. His published works include *L'Eglise et les religions non-chrétiennes* (Mulhouse, 1967) and *"Pour un renouveau du dialogue judéo-chrétien,"* in *Bulletin de l'Amitié Judéo-chrétienne de France* 3/4 (1966).

HILDEGARD GOSS-MAYR: Born in Austria in 1930, she studied philology, history and philosophy at Vienna and in America at New Haven, receiving her doctorate in 1953. She has traveled in Latin America, particularly in Brazil in 1962 with the group called The International Fellowship of Reconciliation. She is editor of the review *Der Christ in der Welt* (Vienna), and will publish this year an account of her experiences in Latin America under the title *Die Macht der Armen.*